A PLUME BOOK

THINK INDIA

VINAY RAI, an engineering graduate from MIT, is a businessman turned academician turned philanthropist and philosopher. He has been an integral part of Indian industry for thirty years, ranking at one time among the top two hundred wealthiest people in the world. Currently, his Rai Foundation has launched university-level schools across India. In the public domain, Rai has promoted many initiatives for women's empowerment, for rural health care, and for the welfare of girls who are orphaned.

A rare example of the practical businessman motivated by a philosophical outlook, Rai is a strong proponent of India's Vedantic heritage that seeks to reconcile the pursuit of concrete business goals and wealth creation with happiness and universal well-being.

WILLIAM L. SIMON is the author or coauthor of more than twenty books, including international bestsellers on subjects ranging from the art of computer hacking, to the building of an interplanetary spacecraft, to *iCon*, a *New York Times* bestselling biography of Steve Jobs. Simon is also a screenwriter, and lives in Los Angeles.

"*Think India* is Vinai Rai's trumpet blast announcing the coming of a new economic superpower. His fascinating book is a must-read for all Americans intrigued by the next wave of seismic economic change."

—Professor Joshua Ronen, Stern School of Business, NYU

"In my fourteen years living and working in India with GE, I learned one big lesson. India is a confusing and difficult place to quickly enact change and make rapid progress. Vinay takes up the classic case of near and yet so far. India sees the goalpost but requires a Herculean leap to get there. This is a must-read for anyone who wants to better understand India."

—Scott R. Bayman, president and CEO of GE India

"The twentieth century belonged to America, but *the twenty-first century belongs to India*. India has everything it takes to be the leading economy in the world. This book explains why . . . but more importantly, how America can prosper as India's most important strategic partner."

—Dr. Richard W. Oliver, CEO of American Sentinel University; board member of several U.S. companies; and author of seven books, including *The Biotech Age: The Business of Biotech and How to Profit from It*

"The astonishing growth of India over the past decade and her emergence on the global stage is an important phenomenon that is not yet widely studied or understood. Vinay Rai and Bill Simon provide a useful and accessible primer on the social, political, geopolitical, and economic landscape of India and look beyond the many challenges and contradictions of our country to reach an unabashedly optimistic assessment of the future."

—Ravi Venkatesan, head of Microsoft Corporation (I) Pvt. Ltd.

"Provides thoughtful insights into many dimensions of this rapidly changing and important country, including Indian culture, business opportunities, government, legal system, religion, and customs."

—Professor Paul L. Joskow, Elizabeth and James Killian Professor of Economics and Management Director, MIT Center for Energy and Environmental Policy Research

"Offers a unique insight into this powerful country's spirit: the most affecting feature that characterizes India's people, and in particular the young ones, is their trust in the future, the courage and willingness to work for it. This book convincingly demonstrates that here, almost unexpectedly, imagination goes along with creative activity, dreamers become successful doers."

—Yvette Biro, Ph.D., professor emeritus at New York University

"This book offers deep insights into how to understand India from one of the most successful and colorful businessmen around. If you can only read one book on India before you visit, this is definitely the one."

—Paul A. Argenti, professor of corporate communication, the Tuck School of Business at Dartmouth

"Provides brilliant insight into the economic explosion, which is transforming not only India but the world. This book should be mandatory reading not only for anyone doing business in India but for all of those who want to understand globalization and the future of the world's economy."

—Lee Bowes, Ph.D.; CEO of America Works

"India has awakened from its centuries-old slumber, heading toward becoming a global superpower. This excellent, beautifully written book presents the unfolding story that every American should know more about."

—Steve Westly, former senior vice president of eBay; California state controller

"Vinay Rai, THINKer and philanthropist, shares his colorful, insightful perspective on his country. His generosity and international business savvy shape this excellent guide to India's past, present, and future."

—Frederic Schwartz, architect of Chennai's new air terminal and founder of the THINK team; and Tracey Hummer, art and architecture writer in New York

The
Rise of the World's
Next Great Power
and What It Means
for Every American

THINK

INDIA

Vinay Rai
and
William L. Simon

A PLUME BOOK

PLUME
Published by the Penguin Group
Penguin Group (USA) Inc., 375 Hudson Street, New York, New York 10014, U.S.A. • Penguin
Group (Canada), 90 Eglinton Avenue East, Suite 700, Toronto, Ontario M4P 2Y3 (a division
of Pearson Penguin Canada Inc.) • Penguin Books Ltd., 80 Strand, London WC2R 0RL,
England • Penguin Ireland, 25 St. Stephen's Green, Dublin 2, Ireland (a division of Penguin
Books Ltd.) • Penguin Group (Australia), 250 Camberwell Road, Camberwell, Victoria 3124,
Australia (a division of Pearson Australia Group Pty. Ltd.) • Penguin Books India Pvt. Ltd.,
11 Community Centre, Panchsheel Park, New Delhi – 110 017, India • Penguin Group (NZ),
67 Apollo Drive, Rosedale, North Shore 0632, New Zealand (a division of Pearson New Zealand
Ltd.) • Penguin Books (South Africa) (Pty.) Ltd., 24 Sturdee Avenue, Rosebank, Johannesburg
2196, South Africa

Penguin Books Ltd., Registered Offices: 80 Strand, London WC2R 0RL, England

Published by Plume, a member of Penguin Group (USA) Inc. Previously published in a Dutton
edition.

First Plume Printing, August 2008
10 9 8 7 6 5 4 3 2 1

Copyright © Vinay Rai and William L. Simon, 2007
All rights reserved

Ⓟ REGISTERED TRADEMARK—MARCA REGISTRADA

The Library of Congress has cataloged the Dutton edition as follows:

Rai, Vinay.
    Think India : the rise of the world's next superpower and what it means for every American
/ by Vinay Rai and William L. Simon.
        p.   cm.
    Includes bibliographical references.
    ISBN 978-0-525-95020-2 (hc.)
    ISBN 978-0-452-28958-1 (pbk.)
    1. India—Economic policy—1991–   2. India—Economic conditions—1991–
3. India—Foreign economic relations.   4. India—Commerce.   I. Simon, William L.,
1930– II. Title.

HC435.3.R34   2007
330.954—dc22
                                                                        2007032309

Printed in the United States of America
Set in A. Caslon
Maps by Jeffrey L. Ward

Without limiting the rights under copyright reserved above, no part of this publication may be reproduced, stored in or introduced into a retrieval system, or transmitted, in any form, or by any
means (electronic, mechanical, photocopying, recording, or otherwise), without the prior written
permission of both the copyright owner and the above publisher of this book.

PUBLISHER'S NOTE
The scanning, uploading, and distribution of this book via the Internet or via any other means
without the permission of the publisher is illegal and punishable by law. Please purchase only au-
thorized electronic editions, and do not participate in or encourage electronic piracy of copy-
righted materials. Your support of the author's rights is appreciated.

BOOKS ARE AVAILABLE AT QUANTITY DISCOUNTS WHEN USED TO PROMOTE PRODUCTS OR SERV-
ICES. FOR INFORMATION PLEASE WRITE TO PREMIUM MARKETING DIVISION, PENGUIN GROUP
(USA) INC., 375 HUDSON STREET, NEW YORK, NEW YORK 10014.

To the New World which one day will be one Family,
to the universal spirit of entrepreneurship,
to Bhagavan Sri Satya Sai Baba, my God, Guru, and Guide,
to my country poised for its new tryst with Destiny
and to my other half, America, always a great open friendly nation
where I spent my most beautiful years as a student.

—VR

And to Arynne, David, Victoria, and Sheldon
and to the memory of my parents, I.B. and Marjorie Simon

—WLS

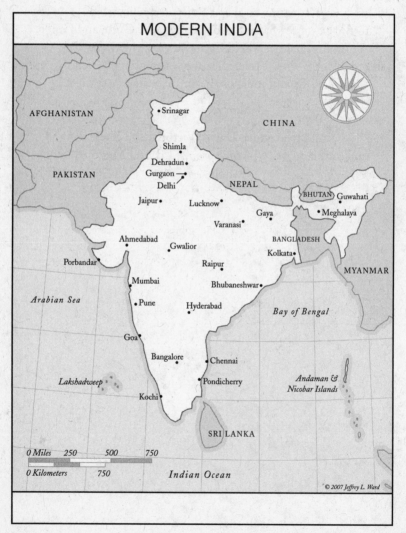

MODERN INDIA

AFGHANISTAN

PAKISTAN

CHINA

NEPAL

BHUTAN · Guwahati
· Meghalaya

BANGLADESH

MYANMAR

· Srinagar

Shimla

Dehradun·
Gurgaon·—·Delhi
· Delhi

Jaipur ·   Lucknow·
                             Gaya ·
                  Varanasi·

Ahmedabad
          · Gwalior
                         Raipur·
Porbandar·   Kolkata·

Mumbai ·
                  Bhubaneshwar·
· Pune   Hyderabad·

Goa·

Bangalore ·   · Chennai
                  · Pondicherry

Kochi ·

Arabian Sea

Bay of Bengal

Lakshadweep

Andaman &
Nicobar Islands

SRI LANKA

0 Miles   250   500   750
0 Kilometers   750

Indian Ocean

© 2007 Jeffrey L. Ward

CONTENTS

INTRODUCTION

Ask any American about India and chances are he'll answer in one of three ways. He may describe a land crowded with the poor, sleeping on sidewalks and begging from tourists, or give his mystic vision of elephants, tigers, and the Taj Mahal. Or he might tell the sad story of a friend or neighbor who was cast off by his company when his department was outsourced to India.

But it's almost sure he'd miss mentioning any of the startling, world-changing tales that this book unveils. There is a new India rising up, and it is going to change the world, from Bollywood to world financial markets, from IT to manufacturing, from services to design. People I meet around the world accept the myth of India as a mystical, poverty-stricken land in some remote corner of the globe. Yet in the India of today, activity in construction, in manufacturing, in innovation, abounds everywhere from large cities to small towns and rural villages. Every sector of the economy, without exception, is growing. And not just growing, but at startling rates that reach fifty to a hundred percent annually.

As an Indian businessman-turned-philanthropist, I have been not just a witness but a player in the extraordinary and unexpected recent history of this country, events that are catapulting India on a fast track from a third world nation to a world leader. (Yes, *leader*).

The explosive force of India on the move is already making itself felt on the international scene. Our gross domestic product, with the highest growth rate in the world after China, is predicted to make India the world's number-three economic power within fifteen years. According to the January 2007 edition of the Goldman Sachs "BRICs Report" (BRICs meaning Brazil, Russia, India, and China), India will *surpass* the GDP of the United States by 2050. That shift, already rapidly under way—fueled by India's youth, on the road to becoming the world's largest population of young people, with a purchasing power that is soaring and with salaries much greater than those of their contemporaries in China—will make this vibrant group the largest potential customers worldwide for consumer goods and services.

I'm reminded of a comment I heard about Dallas, Texas, in the boom days of oil exploration—that you didn't dare go to dinner with a banker unless you were prepared to let him loan your company money. That's what it's like in India today. Venture capital and investment capital from around the world are now chasing the Indian entrepreneur; companies and enterprising individuals with promising ideas don't lack for funds.

For American businesses, India, instead of posing a threat, in fact offers remarkable new opportunities. Rather than a place to which the United States is losing jobs, India is unexpectedly emerging as a vital partner to the United States in creating the greener pastures of a new world economy.

America's indomitable spirit to move ahead and its pioneer mentality that inspired the settling of the American West, the landing of men on the moon, and the exploration of Mars is now looking toward the Indian subcontinent as the new frontier. This new India, a vibrant, fast-moving, dynamic, innovative country, shares more qualities with America than any other nation on earth. Both countries honor liberal values of individual enterprise, freedom of expression, multiculturalism, and free markets. Both are democracies committed to a peaceful and prosperous world order through the unleashing of individual creativity. In many ways the world today belongs to the entrepreneurs, the innovators, the dreamers, and the wealth creators. In that, Americans are unbeatable . . . but so are the new young Indians.

And these aren't the only reasons to "Think India" when you picture the next great superpower: India and not Japan, or Brazil, or the European Union, or even the country that most often pops to mind, China. India's people—diverse, open, practical, innovative, and service-oriented—are the country's real strength. Their creative energies, unleashed after hundreds of years of slavery and foreign rule, are driving modern India to new heights.

Think India paints a startling new image of economic advancement and potential as it unravels the great enigma that is India. With over seven thousand years of history and cultural diversity, Indians are quite a complex lot—a mixture of contrasting cultures rubbed together through centuries of contact, bonded by common spiritual threads, in tune with the wisdom of life and the art of well-being.

You cannot visit India today without sensing a nation on the move. A feeling of abundance and optimism combined with a belief in India's destiny pervades all walks of life. India has all the resources—land, water, oil and gas, coal, minerals—and is driving forward to take its place among the leading nations of the world. It is already one of the fastest-growing markets for American products; by 2020 *one-half* of the world population of people under age twenty-five will be here in India! Their new spending power will make India the biggest cash-drawer worldwide for consumer goods and services.

I'm fortunate to have moved among the richest of the rich worldwide—at the World Economic Forums at Davos and elsewhere during my travels—and also among the poorest of the poor as a phi-lanthropist in education. The emerging India I introduce you to in this book is viewed through the lens of my personal experiences in business and my interactions over so many years with leaders in poli-tics, government, religion, and the corporate world.

Chapter 1 provides an overview of India today, followed by a chapter that lays out the amazing story of how a nation only lately re-covered from being under the thumb of the Soviets came to be the home of an IT and outsourcing revolution that has spearheaded an economic growth almost unparalleled in the history of the world.

Chapter 3 looks at the glowing face of India's finance capital, Mumbai, and the fairy tale of its bizarre growth. In Chapter 4, I ex-plore how India's seven-thousand-year history shapes the thinking and attitudes of Indians today. In Chapter 5, I examine the crucial role of India in the United States' global "war on terror" and as an effective counterbalance to the growing threat of a potentially menacing China. The following chapter, "India's Growing Global Muscle," looks at the impact locally as India, for the first time in over a thousand years, struts on the global stage; I also lay out the reasons why it will be In-dia, not China, that will become the foremost partner of American business. The Chinese see a business relationship in the short term, lasting only until it has served its purpose; the businesspeople of India want to form a relationship first and do business afterward—looking at the long term.

Before you deal with a stranger, you'd like to know something about his character; Chapter 7 unveils the paradoxes of the Indian personality—the nature of these multidimensional, multitasking, multiprocessing, highly innovative entrepreneurial minds. Chapter 8 turns to the incomparable landscape and peoples of India, which, af-ter decades of being a destination only for the truly adventurous or spiritual, is now receiving swarms of tourists, business visitors, and, of all things, people looking for world-class but inexpensive medical procedures, from a new set of uppers, to open-heart surgery, to getting rid of wrinkles. Whatever the reason that draws them, most stay to take in the experiences and sights of this ancient civilization.

While the promise of India's future seems unlimited, so does the magnitude of its problems. There are so very many poor that the resources to give them even a basic security of subsistence-level living stands as a mountainous challenge. In Chapter 9, I examine what India is doing today to solve the seemingly unsolvable.

The book concludes with a look at the India of tomorrow, sharing the thinking of strategists and planners from around the world of the day when India has economically drawn abreast of the United States.

For Americans, India as a new frontier carries the hope that mankind may truly be moving toward the dream of one world based upon the ideal of harmony—a world that recognizes the oneness of humanity and where religion no longer divides people, no longer serves as a justification for acts of violence and destruction in the name of God.

In today's world, national boundaries remain only for the weak-hearted. The great seekers of wealth look beyond boundaries and nationalities.

India welcomes these seekers to its shores.

THINK

India is the only millionaire—the One land that all men desire to see, and having seen once, by even a glimpse, would not give that glimpse for all the shows of all the rest of the globe combined.

—Mark Twain, in *Following the Equator*

CHAPTER 1

WELCOME TO INDIA

To the visitor rolling into Delhi just before dawn, the only visible landscape is fog-tangled trees and quiet shadows. The early morning mist, hanging like a soft shawl over crumbling fifteenth-century walls, lush gardens, and the white-domed tombs of long-ago sultans, magically blocks out eyesores.

Through its soft gauze the capital appears a placid, lost-in-time place where the romance of Kubla Khan, Kim, and the Koh-I-Noor diamond lives on. Those who set foot here may be lured by India's glittering gems or software genius, pulled by couture fashions turning heads on runways or by ancient monuments and tales of genies and dervishes; they may arrive unveiling blueprints for new factories and drug research centers; they may head to mountaintop ashrams or check into hospitals to be nipped and tucked. But whether gazing out from bus windows or shaded limos, all who peer into the tranquil dawn that envelops the sleeping metropolis—where there's little sign of life at this hour save for monkeys scrambling along high walls—have cause to wonder if they have slipped into an entirely different world.

Indeed, they have.

As the sun rises over this northern city of thirteen million that holds the government seat of the world's largest democracy, it's quickly obvious to visitors that they are caught in a reality warp where the only norm is extremes and every day is a blur of bright colors, nonstop honking, and drifting scents of curries, regularly punctuated by car wrecks and electrical blackouts. In a country with over one billion residents and a booming economy that is suddenly putting a million new cars on the road every year, India is home to what could be the world's worst urban congestion as the people of this vibrant culture—now globally lauded for producing IT whizzes, engineers, scientists, authors, and economists—parade by its window.

One-quarter of the world's poor live in India, and it is impossible to exist in the country without being constantly aware of the great divide of wealth among the people one passes on the street. Heaving trucks painted in screaming pinks and greens jostle for space with bicycle rickshaws and sputtering open-air three-wheeler taxis that zip

A few elephants join rush hour traffic in central Delhi.   (*Idris Ahmed*)

past the occasional trumpeting elephant, perhaps even a sauntering camel or two with turbaned boys riding atop. Women in flowing scarves and brilliantly hued silk saris ride sidesaddle on the backs of motorcycles, weaving past sidewalk dentists stringing up their pliers, past roadside barbers hammering their mirrors onto trees for that day's shaves, past office buildings with familiar logos such as IBM and GE. Toothpick-legged beggars run out at red lights to press their maimed toddlers against car windows, pointing at the child's missing hands, which the parents themselves may have cut off. All of this can be seen on just a few miles of road through Delhi.

Still, Indians rich or poor are largely a thoughtful, tranquil bunch who may reference the past life and the next one as casually as speaking of yesterday and tomorrow—reflecting the Hindu belief in Karma and Destiny, teachings that say our acts of today will be reflected in the next life and our acts of the past will define today's life. These beliefs lend a sense of stability to every day in even the most trying of times. In microcosm, you can see examples of this on the roadways constantly: India could rightly be called "the land of the blaring horn"—trucks are even required to have painted on their rear panels the request for passing vehicles to BLOW HORN, but Indians are notorious honkers even without the invitation. Yet when traffic backs up, the cacophony quickly ceases as the drivers patiently wait for whatever caused this jam to be cleared up or sorted out.

Shocking, startling India—where one may easily experience the entire gamut of emotions from sheer bliss to horror in the course of an hour—is not one country but many Indias all locked into one geographical place. These diverse lands aren't even bound to the same century, despite the calendar's date: here, where the word *bullish* is tossed around by slick urban economists, futures analysts, and foreign investors plowing into this market, about a quarter of the country's residents live in lean-tos or thatch huts where their entire fortunes may be invested in their plow-pulling bullocks.

While India is finalizing plans with the United States for sending a man to the moon, a villager's concept of the universe doesn't extend much beyond the forest where she spends half the day gathering twigs, carried back on her head as that night's fuel; asked about what she thinks of the changes revolutionizing the country, she shrugs. "Is it changing? How would I know?"

It's simply not possible to describe "average" or "normal" in this country: the landscape varies from swirling deserts to ice-capped mountains so forbidding they defy the building of roads; from the soft mountains of the Eastern Ghats, thick with teak trees and orchids, to the south's flat, boulder-strewn Deccan Plateau that yields India's diamonds and gold; from impenetrable jungles untouched by civilization to soft sand beaches bursting with tourist hotels.

Until 1947, there was no formal country of India, and even when occasionally united under assorted empires, the landmass was split into hundreds of kingdoms and principalities; as a result modern India is easily likened to Europe, with disparities between neighboring lands as vast as those between Germany and France—so different from the United States, with its homogeneous culture, unchanging even as you cross state lines. Disparities in India abound even in the spoken word: traveling the country, one encounters dozens of entirely different languages, in many cases written with different alphabets. It's said in India that one need travel only fifty miles to uncover an entirely new world.

Across this country, where the officially outlawed caste system may still dictate one's destiny from birth, traffic becomes the great equalizer, bringing the masses together in one shared concrete reality for miles at a time. It matters little if a person is a high-caste Brahmin or a Dalit—

an "untouchable" so low on the pole that until recently they wore bells to signal their arrival and could be killed for touching the water well—regardless of whether they're one of the country's over seventy thousand millionaires or the dozens of billionaires whose names top *Forbes* lists, or if they're that quarter of the country that survives on less than a dollar a day, they're all here on the road, often stuck in a traffic jam.

Every sixth person on earth resides in India, providing a vast, eager, youthful workforce that is a lure for foreign manufacturers drawn by new incentives—including low-tax zones—to set up factories here.

On the culture side, the country is churning out startlingly gifted scribes—Arundhati Roy *(The God of Small Things)*, Kiran Desai *(The Inheritance of Loss)*, and Salman Rushdie *(Midnight's Children)* all took Britain's prestigious Booker Prize; V. S. Naipaul and Amartya Sen won Nobels, and Vikram Chandra, Raj Kamal Jha, and Vikram Seth are but a few illustrating the Indian flair for English that is the legacy of the British Empire. On the flip side, four hundred million Indians—some say far more—can't read any language whatsoever; a mere sixty-five percent of Indians are literate . . . and this in a country where the definition of literacy officially means nothing more than to be able to write your own name.

In this land that Europeans once called Hindustan, religion is another major hallmark of diversity. Eighty-one percent of the population are Hindus, but India is also home to some 140 million Muslims—the world's largest Muslim population outside of Indonesia. Millions more are Sikhs, Buddhists, Jainists, Christians, or Zoroastrians. Hindus don't eat beef, Muslims don't eat pork, almost half of the population is entirely vegetarian, and peaceful Jainists won't even eat root vegetables out of concern for the welfare of the plant.

Hindus and Buddhists embrace astrology, consulting the planets on matters from gem buying to weddings; Muslims and Sikhs shun it.

Men in cities tend towards store-bought Western clothes, although in villages they may wear the printed wraps called loongi. While college students may be equally comfortable in jeans, many women, young and old, including those holding high positions in the corporate world, are often clad in saris or chic tunics with matching pants, and many still veil their heads when in the presence of elders. No wonder the country's ethos is "Unity in diversity" and "Diversity in unity"— and those are more than PR lines.

It's an understatement to say that India can be overwhelming: whether looking out onto the verdant terraced fields that tumble down from the Himalayas in the north, gasping at the incredible stone and tile artwork of an imposing eighth-century cliff-top fort perched over central India's now-forgotten kingdom of Gwalior, or drinking in the breathtaking design of the Taj Mahal, it becomes quickly obvious that the only common thread here is complexity.

In 1991, when the Soviet Union, then India's main trading partner, came crashing down, the Indian finance minister, who was a respected economist, made a controversial move that is now credited with saving India's economy and boosting it to heights never dreamed of before. He daringly liberalized India, switching the economy's design from a tightly closed socialist model in which the state owned most large enterprises, discouraged entrepreneurship, overregulated everything, and stifled foreign investment, to an economy that ran more on free market rules. He creaked open the door to foreign investment and encouraged India's entrepreneurs to launch new businesses. Critics, led by the Communists and socialists, denounced the policies, but they've shut up now: since 1991, the GDP has doubled.

This rapid swelling of the economy has elicited more than expressions of surprise worldwide: it has also put more change into the

pockets of Indians, whose per capita income has been increasing between four and five percent a year. There are now more Indian millionaires than British millionaires. With figures showing that Indians
are spending billions for luxury goods, high-end retailers such as
Cartier and Gucci are hightailing it to India to set up shop in five-star
hotels or swanky new shopping centers.

According to *Forbes*, the richest forty people in India had a collec-
tive worth of over $61 billion in 2004; by 2007—this time for only 36
people—the figure had jumped to a startling $191 billion. Another
result of the explosive economic growth: the rise of a middle class—
some estimates put the number as high as three hundred million—
each member boasting disposable income, virgin credit cards, and a
hankering for shopping malls.

India's huge parallel economy—money or assets that are not declared or on which no taxes are paid, termed the black economy—
means that the official figures greatly understate the reality. Rumor
has it that just taking into account the real value of the houses and
property Indians own in India and abroad would easily add a few *million* millionaires, and a few hundred billionaires. These numbers
alone boggle the mind.

In geopolitics, India has overnight soared in stature from "nuclear
delinquent" to strategic political, military, and economic partner; the
same G-8 countries that wagged their fingers earlier are now hailing
India as a responsible nuclear power and stumbling over each other in
a race to supply India's nuclear fuel to electrify her countryside. The
benchmark year was 2006: President George W. Bush, former president Bill Clinton, French president Jacques Chirac, Russian president
Vladimir Putin, Saudi king Abdullah, China's premier, and the president of Austria all touched down in Delhi—which was busy making
a gas deal with Iran, an oil exploration deal with China, and a nuclear

energy deal with the United States. The visits of these political glit-
terati beamed the spotlight on India as they lauded her unleashed
potential, intellectual leaders, and efforts to address the country's
staggering poverty, while heartily welcoming the country into the
close-knit club of international hotshots.

The press forgot China for months: India snagged the covers of
hundreds of international magazines—*Time, Newsweek, The Economist, National Geographic Traveler,* even design magazine *Wallpaper.*
With the media now on "India Watch," the country once synony-
mous with fly-covered children and Mother Teresa is consistently
snatching top headlines, this time cast as an innovator and rising star.

"Our two great democracies," announced President George W.
Bush during his landmark visit in March 2006, "are now united by
opportunities that can lift our people, and by threats that can bring
down all our progress. The United States and India, separated by half
the globe, are closer than ever before, and the partnership between
our free nations has the power to transform the world." As he left, the
president vowed to pressure Congress to loosen any restrictions that
impeded the country's new friendship, burgeoning trade, and growing
ties in defense.

The U.S.-India alliance is in part a military extension of the U.S.-
led "war on terror": since 2002, the two countries have been running
extensive joint military exercises—from fleet maneuvers in the Indian
Ocean to coordinated air force drills in the mountainous terrains of
Alaska and India. The other aspect of that partnership is economic:
while Indian companies hope to elevate their global presence, American companies want to cash in on the growing consumer market as
well as the massive projects of electrifying the country and building
nuclear power plants. General Electric alone is forecasting that its
business in India could top $3 billion in 2007.

Another potentially loud clinking in American piggybanks comes from an ongoing revamp of India's military arsenal. India is shopping for 120 fighter planes—and Lockheed Martin and Boeing (which recently sold $11 billion worth of aircraft to Air India) are elbowing each other to land that multibillion-dollar deal, the biggest of the century.

As I'll show in more detail, this partnering likely has political motives as well, as a means by which both countries can counterbalance China's growing economic and military might. Nobody in either government has yet explicitly acknowledged this motive, but the logic is clear.

"The new alliance between the U.S. and India," says Ron Somers, who heads the influential U.S.-Indian Business Council that brings together two hundred of the top American and Indian companies, "is going to change the face of the twenty-first century." For starters, it looks to bring a lot more cash into both countries' economies; Somers has predicted that doing business in India will pour over a trillion dollars into American business coffers by 2025.

Yet another bond between the two countries is the "Indian diaspora," the overseas pilgrimage of scientists, engineers, academicians, physicians, and other professionals. Locally called NRIs, for "nonresident Indians," about a million of these voyagers live in the U.S. alone, many as creators or leaders of young companies. A growing political force, the hard-lobbying NRIs in the United States helped trigger the two governments to form the new U.S.-India alliance.

Indians abroad have unleashed revolutionary new inventions (the creation of the famous Pentium chip by Vinod Dahm and the invention of Hotmail by Sabeer Bhatia are but two). They also send back billions to India—over $23 billion in 2007, representing an astounding three percent of the country's GDP—and they are crucial in founding new enterprises in India as well as outsourcing work to India.

But for all the optimism, the plans in the works, the excitement, India's economic surge and rising global stature haven't yet reached the millions of villagers whose only water, pumped from the communal spigot, is usually polluted, and whose shabby crops don't yield enough to sustain them. As we shall see in some detail, the problems of the rural poor represent some of the gravest challenges for the Indian government and society, a need being addressed on many fronts yet leaving much still to be done.

Beneath all the too-obvious problems and causes for concern, a certain quiet but strong sense of happiness and belief in the future pervades India and Indians—a sentiment that Westerners may find perplexing. Give even a wealthy man a simple dish of spicy lentils and a stack of the rounds of soft, puffy bread known as poori and he delves in with relish, philosophizing about the importance of experiencing joy in everyday life.

As India moves toward being accepted as a major player among the world's nations, the people of the country are changing their outlook. A group president of the telecom giant Reliance, Tony Jesudasan, who previously worked at the U.S. Embassy in Delhi, describes the shift by saying, "Twenty years ago, everybody wanted to get out of India. The upper class and the upper middle class all sent their kids abroad to be educated." But, Jesudasan says, "you don't see that so much anymore. And in the old days, when I talked to kids, they always wanted to know how they could get a U.S. visa, even if that meant becoming a cabdriver in New York or working at a pizza place. That's changing. Now people want to stay in India. There are jobs here."

In a reversal that would have been unthinkable just a decade or two ago, Indians living abroad are returning, in what some of the locals have taken to calling a "reverse brain drain." Indian scientists, doctors, engineers, and managers are coming back to the country. The mood is buoyant, in the cities at least, where there's an elation that is almost palpable.

The confidence and dynamism of the Indian people is compelling. The foreigner who steps on Indian soil cannot but be amazed by the level of activity, the sheer dynamism of a nation on the move.

"People used to say that we were doomed," says Jesudasan, "that it was the fate of India to be poor and starving and devastated by droughts and floods. People believed that was India's destiny, our Karma. Now you don't hear the negative words, only a great confidence about the future. The new generation lives in the firm belief that the best is yet to come."

CHAPTER 2

WHAT MAKES INDIA CLICK?

A Nation's Unparalleled Growth

Setting: Bangalore, India's Silicon Valley

The simple ground-level sign, not even half the size of a typical billboard, doesn't exactly jump out, being just another sight among the potholes of Hosur Road in the southern city of Bangalore, where the noisy weave of cars and trucks, rickshaws and ox-pulled wagons, mirrors the chaos of transportation in every other Indian city. The understated appearance of this red-lettered ELECTRONICS CITY marker is deceptive, however, since it symbolizes a very big deal: turning right off Hosur Road at this sign, one leaves behind the honking and the hawkers peddling trinkets and enters India's future. What lies before you is the two-square-mile area that catapulted not just Bangalore but the whole country onto the world scene, forever altering India's reputation and earning potential—and blowing up a whirlwind of economic, geopolitical, and social change that is still reshaping the country in ways few previously fathomed even possible.

Lined with low-draping trees and dripping with flowers, this smooth-paved ribbon of road unfurls past 332 acres of immaculately landscaped grounds dotted with striking architectural designs: a glass pyramid here, a circular spaceship there, buildings designed like billowing sails or folded like origami. Belying the serene surroundings, Electronics City—an industrial park that's now home to over a hundred electronics and software firms—is the dynamic epicenter of twenty-first-century India: this is the portal that linked the country with the world market, and propelled the subcontinent, in terms of technology at least, to the farthest reaches of modernity.

Behind these dense hedges, a high-tech revolution has been brewing for over two decades, its pace accelerating to a breakneck speed in the past few years. What's powered this revolution, and the object of fascination for India's brightest employed here—engineers to software designers, most in their twenties—can be summed up with the two letters *IT*. Information technology is now at the core of day-to-day life, running everything from your computer and cell phone to almost every facet of every company's activities. The electronic magic carpet of IT has glided into a trillion-dollar industry and has

Convergys's headquarters in Electronics City—just one of numerous multinational corporations set up in Bangalore   (*Hindustan Times*)

spawned commerce worldwide that has brought in trillions more. It was IT that helped India get its groove back—bringing confidence, accolades, global recognition, and a prosperity for India unlike anything ever imagined.

In July 1981, nobody knew that Narayana Murthy was creating an industry; at that precarious moment, Murthy himself wasn't even sure he was launching a viable company. A manager for a Mumbai firm that resold giant American computers to a handful of Indian businesses, Murthy walked out one day with six of his underlings. India, they realized, was hopelessly behind the times; most of the country's few computers were the monstrous contraptions that took up entire rooms. Meanwhile, in the United States, new unbelievably small computers, soon to be widely known as PCs, were beginning to take off.

Murthy and his coworkers realized that these new machines would revolutionize American business. They also realized that few people anywhere on the planet had the skills needed to help businesses figure out how to manage and integrate their PCs.

The young engineers had at least a modicum of computer skills, so they decided to take advantage of a new, illogical law declaring that only small companies would be granted the right to work with computers. A few weeks later, Infosys was born, with Murthy at its head and a plan in hand to reap riches from the West, where businesses, they were convinced, needed their help.

From the start, Infosys faced problems, big problems, among them the fact that Murthy and his colleagues—whose yearly pay had ranged from one thousand to five thousand dollars—had no money to invest. Banks laughed them out the door when they applied for even small loans; potential investors had no idea what they were even talking about. Murthy finally borrowed $250 from his wife and set about trying to get the company a license—a process of spending entire days waiting in line for a stamp here, another stamp there, stretching into weeks.

But Murthy finally emerged with the necessary paperwork—and as soon as Infosys sent out feelers to the United States, companies began to nibble. The time had come to increase staff; the first employees were rather aghast to discover that their office was Murthy's small guestroom in the back of his tiny apartment. The next hurdle came, as usual, from the government, which didn't like Indian businesses working abroad and required that they be given official permission for overseas business trips. It took months of jumping through all sorts of hoops, but the bureaucrats finally granted permission for a few Infosys guys to head to the United States to design new software for American businesses. The result of these early efforts, twenty-six years later, is an Infosys empire with sixty-seven thousand employees worldwide and revenues of over $2 billion in 2006.

I was another of those who took a chance on jumping into the technology business, with my MIT engineering education in electronics and computer science as a confidence builder in taking the gamble. I developed tie-ins with two small entrepreneurial companies in California, Alpha Micro and Eagle Computers, and arranged to buy computer parts from them—processors, memory, display screens, keyboards, and so on. Company heads like me spent days on end shuttling from the Ministry of Electronics, to the Ministry of Industry, to the Ministry of Commerce, trying to get the needed licenses to import materials, licenses to manufacture, licenses to produce so many units. Most officials did not understand this new sector. I found the banks had no idea whether it was safe to lend rupees to a company offering virtually no assets beyond its intellectual capital, and IT was not even recognized as an industry with any local history for predicting the likelihood of success.

But finally, with enough patience and enough "gifts" to bureaucrats, we were able to start importing components, which we then assembled and began to sell in the Indian market, making us the first company to offer PCs in India. Those were exciting days for us, the pioneers, when creativity in the face of challenges was the order of the day.

Throughout the 1980s and 1990s, other high-tech companies were starting to spring up, but not nearly enough to provide jobs for the flood of engineers who graduated each year from India's premier colleges. At least a fifth of those graduates slipped off to the United States, where they found rapid employment in Silicon Valley; some in India muttered that the national government was subsidizing America's industry. But the brain drain had two very positive effects: It helped stamp the idea on the world that Indians were cutting-edge engineers. And once those Indians rose to high positions, many began slashing costs in their projects by subcontracting work to firms in India.

Then, as the 1990s drew to a close, the world's industrial nations started waking up to the computer problems that would threaten as soon as the calendar rolled over to 2000. (Early computer programmers had allowed only two digits for the year; a calculation for the span of time from 1958 to 1962 involved the simple arithmetic of 62 minus 58. Now use that same calculation for the span from 1998 to 2002; the program follows the same rules, calculating 02 minus 98 and kicking out an answer of 96 years. Every single computer program that used dates would have to be examined and rewritten.) With the Y2K programming effort looking like it would require the services of vastly more computer programmers than were available in all the industrialized countries put together, the media foretold gloomily that the glitch would bring down everything from dams, to high-rise elevators, to the systems that kept giant corporations running. All eyes started turning toward India, where companies offering programming services were standing at the ready. Y2K gave the Indian technology industry that last little kick-start it needed to really set the economy aloft.

CEOs who before hadn't had much need for India began frantically dialing the 91 country code as the millennium approached. Thousands of American companies began desperately shoveling money at companies like Wipro and Infosys, causing IT revenues to reach amounts never before dreamed of. By then, it wasn't just software companies that were riding the wave. India's economy was lighting up across the board, with orders and investments rolling in from all corners, while new high-rises and office towers shot up across the land. And it wasn't just call centers and back-office work like filling out tax forms—although indeed those business were going gangbusters.

Whatever the cause—globalization, newfound pride, India finally landing in the focus of the international spotlight—the IT boom was the spark that caused a tremendous economic explosion all across the country. As more factories opened, infrastructure began to improve, while everybody from high-end luxury retailers to breakfast-food makers barreled in to tap the expanding Indian wallet.

What's peculiar is how this dynamic growth—now over eight percent a year, and exceeding all forecasts—defies traditional economic development: every other country has always advanced its agriculture, then small-scale commerce, then moved to manufacturing, then on to high-end services. "In India we reversed the cycle," notes R. Gopalakrishnan, executive director of Tata Sons Limited. "We started with high-value services, moved to high-value manufactured goods, and now are looking at improving infrastructure, and no one has yet a clue on agriculture improvement. Indian growth has gone against all common conventional wisdom."

And just as odd was that all systems were blinking green simultaneously. "In the rest of the world, some sectors are going up while some are going down," notes Gopalakrishnan. "Surprisingly, in India, *all* sectors are booming. Nothing is slowing down. There is no fading industry."

These early companies were cheered on by renowned consulting firm McKinsey and Company, whose reports continually lauded India's young IT industry and gave it international credence. The stampede began, with thousands of Western companies jumping into the action.

But the phenomenon didn't remain confined to Bangalore. Corporate giant Tata Group jumped into technology with Tata Consultancy Services, TCS, based in Mumbai; its revenues are now over $5 billion. These firms and hundreds of others that gambled early saw their dreams turn to gold. And in some cases, not just for the owners but for the workers as well—an idea fresh and surprising in India. Infosys, for one, offered employees stock in the company: now hundreds of the early workers are multimillionaires, while Wipro's head man, Azim Premji, topped Indians on the *Forbes* list of billionaires for nearly a decade.

The innovations flying out of Bangalore opened up myriad new enterprises and spinoffs—from customer-service call centers to outsourced legal and medical work. Lawyers in New York and L.A. who began sending digital recordings via e-mail to India would walk into their offices the next morning to find the transcription waiting—for half the price and in a fraction of the time it would normally take. Following their lead, hospitals began sending X-rays to India for preliminary diagnosis.

All of this outsourcing resulted in some unexpected changes for the average Indian. Call centers promising 24/7 response meant shifts for Indian workers with hours that might be eight P.M. to five A.M. The foreign companies signing on for these services had no idea they were triggering social changes a world away: rarely had Indian men and women worked side by side through the night. And suddenly recent college grads were making more money than their parents.

This IT success story boosted India's sagging morale and drastically altered its international image, putting it on the front lines of twenty-first-century science, engineering, and technology. IT, says marketing research guru Arvind Singhal of Technopak, "branded India internationally as a source of innovation and excellence." His words are echoed widely in reports from the U.S. government to reports from the World Bank.

If the world was shocked that a land thought of in terms of its sacred cows and its mountaintop gurus was proving itself a source of innovative technology and engineering prowess, the news came as little

Young men and women working in an Indian call center, servicing
international clients   (*Hindustan Times*)

surprise to anyone armed with knowledge of the history of science, where Indian names are well known. Physicist Sir Jagadish Chandra Bose worked in the late 1800s and early 1900s with electromagnetic waves and became the first Indian to nab a U.S. patent, helping to lay the foundation for modern radio. Another major figure of the same last name, Satyendra Nath Bose, after being shot down by scientific academies for his bizarre findings about energy particles, took his research to Albert Einstein, who embraced the Indian's revolutionary insights and incorporated them into quantum physics; together the pair developed what is still known as Bose-Einstein statistics.

Physicist C. V. Raman's insights into the nature of light garnered him the Nobel Prize for physics in 1938, and his nephew, astrophysicist Subramanyan Chandrasekhar, broke new ground in the understanding of distant stars, pioneering such concepts as white dwarves and black holes, for which he took the Nobel Prize for physics in 1983. Other Indian scientists designed and put a satellite in space in 1974, a spacecraft that incorporated much of their own work.

In part because of this tradition of scientific know-how, in 2004, McKinsey predicted that major global corporations would be keen to park their investments for R & D facilities in India rather than China. Their crystal ball proved accurate. As I write, in early 2007, there are already some two hundred R & D labs in India churning out intellectual property. While the Intel team is busy developing microprocessor chips for wireless broadband technology, engineers at GE's John F. Welch Technology Centre in Bangalore are developing innovative solutions for aircraft engines and transport. Around India, signs on office buildings and factories carry names like ACNielsen, Microsoft, Motorola, Pfizer, Novartis, and Eli Lilly.

Once IT and IT-enabled services catapulted India onto the global stage, the rest of the world quickly noticed India's vast pool of intellectual human resources. Even if the accents ring with a different lilt and vowel sound, for many Indians, English is a native tongue spoken from birth, along with at least one or two other of India's many languages. Indian universities, led by campuses of the Indian Institute of Technology and the Indian Institute of Management, are turning out a whole new class of English-speaking researchers, innovators, managers, and entrepreneurs.

The effect of this growth on the Indian consumer is evident anywhere you travel in the country. Until a few years ago, India had only a few automated teller machines, but today they can be seen almost anywhere. Mobile phones—the now-essential tool of the global business player—have found a bonanza of new subscribers in India's suddenly flush population, as Indians snatch up cell phones even faster than the Chinese do. In 2005 alone, thirty-two million handsets were sold in India.

Is the World Really Flat?

Impelled by India's success on the IT landscape, in 2004 *New York Times* columnist Thomas Friedman blew through the town of Bangalore with an investigative team for the Discovery Channel to uncover what all the hubbub was about. His final interview was with Nandan Nilekani, one of Infosys's seven original founders. What was happening, Nilekani told Friedman on camera, was that thanks to globalization, "the playing field [of the whole world] is being leveled."

From there, Friedman leapt to the theory offered up in his runaway bestselling *The World Is Flat*. His basic premise: The ever-increasing access to technology and communications is leading to a flattening in which the industrialized nations no longer have a significant advantage. The world becomes a level playing field.

When you look at the growth rate for the booming technology sector in India, you almost agree with Friedman: the Indian IT/outsourcing segment blasted through at a growth rate averaging forty-two percent over the last two fiscal years.

But if technology alone is the great enabler, as Friedman would have us believe, why haven't other nations—most of them having the possibility of the same kind of access to Internet connectivity—reaped the benefit? Why aren't countries like Spain, Italy, Poland, Pakistan, Sri Lanka, Argentina, or Malaysia enjoying the same kind of growth?

What's more, IT isn't the only growth area for India. How would Friedman account for India's huge growth curve in sectors as diverse as world-class manufacturing, design, engineering, aviation, telecom, health care, real estate, retail, movies, and entertainment? Or if indeed there is a flattening at work in India and China, then why are large parts of both these nations still poor and the gap between rich and poor continuing to widen? Moreover, in this flat world, where jobs are flowing easily from New York to New Delhi, why is it that income levels are not becoming flat simultaneously?

Accepting Friedman's hypothesis of information technology as the great equalizer simply doesn't explain India's outperforming the rest of the don't-have nations. A country's growth and achievement spring from far more complex reasons. Technology isn't even an "enabler" unless people at the user end of the equation are inventive in the day-to-day situations of ordinary life. A shining illustration: the efficient use of computers, telephones, and Internet search engines by people in some remote Indian villages, some of whom can't even properly write their own names.

Friedman, to his credit, does mention—though only in passing—the creation of India's seven Indian Institute of Technology centers that have kick-started a phenomenal knowledge meritocracy in India. "It's like a factory, churning out and exporting some of the most gifted engineering, computer science, and software talent on the globe," Friedman writes. He acknowledges the importance of this "people power" as a steady supply of brainpower "from New Delhi to Palo Alto" and as one of the root causes of the Indian outsourcing revolution. Yet he doesn't see this root factor as a reason that India's success doesn't fit into his "flat world" formula.

With due apologies to Friedman, then, it would be too simplistic to assume that software, uploading, outsourcing, offshoring, supply-chaining, in-sourcing, and the rest of Friedman's "ten forces that flat-tened the world" are the only reasons for the rise of Asian countries. The answer: Technology alone does not make every part of the world equal. Access to technology in itself does not guarantee the creative health of a people. The theory holds water only when the culture thrives with certain essential characteristics: an inquiring attitude and an emphasis on education.

Add India's legendary innovative ability and entrepreneurship acu-men to those skill sets, and what you have is a root explanation for the gravity-defying success that Indian IT has been racking up. Wipro vice president A. Vasudevan lays the bouquet at the feet of the eight and a half million who earn bachelor degrees every year, the half-million engineering graduates, and the twelve thousand Ph.D.'s.

In short, a technology inherits, a people invent.

For India, it is not technology alone that's unleashing the potential of her people. Culture, values, leadership, entrepreneurship, educa-tion, innovation, social responsibility, cohesion, and communication are all critical ingredients. India's democratic society, combined with a supportive regulatory environment, are key to propelling her north-ward along the growth highway.

No wonder India today is rubbing shoulders with the first world, while Pakistan and Bangladesh and a large number of countries in Africa and South America, despite the so-called "flattening" effect of technology, still have a long way to go.

I strongly believe that it is India's competitive advantage on the high-end value chain in manufacturing—compared to China's competitive edge in the low-margin goods—that will drive India ahead of China as a global player. The day is coming when mass-consumption products will be conceived in the United States, designed in India, manufactured in China, sold globally, and serviced by India and the United States jointly for the global market.

Defying the "Flatness" Fundamentals: The Indian Concept of Jugaad

The sun that rises over the city of Mumbai each day of the work-week beams down on morning preparations for what must be without question one of the most unusual delivery systems anywhere in the world, one that illustrates India's unique aptitude for problem solving: the dabbawaalahs ("dabba" for lunch box, "waalah" for person), who have become the stuff of folklore.

In a city where, despite burgeoning populations and growing mod-ernization, thousands of people still prefer to eat homemade lunch—because the food is both fresher and less expensive—over 175,000 box lunches are carried every day from a worker's own house to his office in a human chain of messengers who travel in shifts by train and bus. Each delivery makes a journey of as much as thirty-five or forty miles from the home kitchen or a Jugaad cooking center to the worker's desk, arriving on time every single day, somehow undeterred by disruptive storms or train breakdowns. With each dabba carrying a home-cooked meal for specific customers, delivery mix-ups would cause mayhem; mostly illiterate, the dabbawaalahs have dreamed up an innovative color-coding system based on acronyms that has made this supply chain virtually foolproof.

The dabbawaalahs are a living definition of an Indian trait we call "Jugaad"—a uniquely Indian practice that can be roughly understood as a solutions-oriented entrepreneurial attitude calling on any conceivable means to reach the desired end. Author Pavan K. Varma, in his book *Being Indian,* cites an example, this one from the state of Punjab. Owners of restaurants along the highway, faced with the need to produce quickly and in quantity a popular ancient frothy drink called lassi, came up with an unexpected use for the home washing machine: Pour in yogurt, sugar, spices, salt, and water, and tap the outflow tube as an exit pipe from which the lassi flows right into glasses ready for serving up to customers. Varma describes this example as a solution "in effortless sync with the ebb and flow of daily life."

"Jugaad," Varma says, "is creative improvisation." He portrays it as a tool to somehow find a solution based on a refusal to accept defeat, and calling on initiative, quick thinking, cunning, and resolve. What qualifies yogurt making as Jugaad is the negligible capital investment and the awesome price-performance relationship. And get this: The dabbawaalah example of Jugaad was honored by *Forbes* magazine with a six-sigma performance rating for efficiency and quality of service, putting a program run by impoverished illiterates on a par with efforts from GE and Motorola.

Indians in the workplace, from one end of the country to the other, rely on the same Jugaad inventiveness for new ways of fulfilling market demands at the lowest possible prices while ensuring the greatest satisfaction, making Jugaad one element in the almost unbelievable growth of today's Indian economy that has left economists scratching their heads, concluding that in economic development, as in most everything else, Indian performance seems to defy expectations and common sense.

A Casebook of Indian-Style Business Visionaries

Every country has its megarich. For a country that so many people still think of in terms of its teeming poor and bedraggled beggars to have many thousands of millionaires, and enough billionaires to be a standout group on the *Forbes* list of the world's richest people, has to stir the curiosity. What is it about the Indian temperament that is producing such vast riches? What are the visionary business qualities that have catapulted these men—and these *women*—to the pedestals of success?

In the early 1950s, when the bureaucratic machinery of India stifled every bit of enterprise and the state controlled every decision, there came a handful of players who would take the stage decades later as key actors in bringing Indian industry into the modern age.

Dhirubhai Ambani—Reliance

After working as a lowly gas station attendant in Dubai, Ambani risked all to come to Mumbai, bringing nothing but his wife and children, his dreams, and an intense desire to become a huge success. He began as a tradesman in textiles until he was able to set up his own small textile company that he called Reliance Manufacturing. Soon

expanding the business to include fibers as well, he followed that success with a series of backward-integration products, leading eventually into what was to become the world's largest oil refinery. The
richest man in India, Dhirubhai gained a foothold in major sectors
including telecom, oil exploration, retail, finance, and investment
banking.

I met this man, whom I always addressed as Dhirubhai ji ("ji" is a
traditional Indian term of respect), as early as 1972 when he was just
another rising star. This was at a time when I had recently joined my
family business after completing my engineering studies at MIT. My
father knew Dhirubhai and suggested I visit him. I immediately
could sense a spark of genius, the sense of a visionary who wanted to
create for himself and for India an unsurpassed economic wealth and
power.

Dhirubhai ji had somehow managed to retain his care for people
and was willing to reach out and help those who asked. I did ask, re-
questing that he become my guide and guru, which he warmly and
generously agreed to do.

Over the years, in my many meetings and discussions with him,
I was always amazed at his realistic, grassroots-level understanding
of the issues involved in India's growth, its politics, and the way forward. He consistently reminded me to remain focused, to buy the
best technology and machinery, hire the best brains, and then produce world-class goods in the most cost-effective way—which I
consider stellar advice for any businessperson, in any industry or
country. Dhirubhai ji always reminded me not to be deflected by
challenges that people or the government throw at businessmen,
and to remain always on track. His sons, Mukesh and Anil, who
now run his businesses, have clearly paid attention to their father's
sage advice.

Dhirubhai, with his great imagination, his knack of going around every possible obstacle, his courage to take on existing lobbies and monopolies, went on consolidating his empire in a way that mirrored the backward-integrated recent growth of India herself.

On his way to megasuccess, Dhirubhai may have been thought to bend some rules, going beyond the ordinary to achieve his out-of-the-box thinking and thus providing tasty meat for the voracious media to rake up controversy. However, Indians are hardly ever scandalized with the Dhirubhai style of rule bending, especially if they see it as being beneficial to the larger society, which this surely was.

Azim Premji—Wipro

Azim Premji was twenty-one, with an electrical engineering degree from Stanford University in California, when his father died. Returning to India for the funeral, Premji discovered that as sole heir he was expected to take over the company. "There's no way a twit like you can run it," one board member snapped at the new CEO during the first meeting he attended. The family business, Western Indian Vegetable Products Limited, dealt in the pressing of oil from peanuts and sunflower seeds.

Premji read up on business and consulted outside experts; he selected only certain types of peanuts for the oil, and he used new equipment to press them. And before too long, the company was showing more profits than it had under his dad. Premji modernized and diversified—later making everything from soaps and creams to light bulbs. And when IBM was rudely ejected from India in 1977, leaving a vacuum in the world of computers—since IBM alone had supplied them—Premji saw his chance to take advantage of the knowledge he had gleaned at Stanford. He shifted the focus but kept the company name, or at least the initials: Wipro.

So what if he didn't know how to make computers and was clueless about software. He marched Wipro into both ventures. Before long Wipro cornered the market for Indian-made computers, and profits poured in.

Although Premji was reigning king of India's computer world, he became weighted down by the endless licenses required for everything, even for taking business trips out of the country. Relief from at least some of the regulatory nonsense came, oddly enough, from the force of oppression itself: the government. When Indira Gandhi was assassinated by her bodyguards in 1984, her liberal son Rajiv Gandhi became premier in a landslide election that was the biggest in India's history. He skewered his own government about the corruption and bureaucracy that he believed killed creativity and slowed progress, and started opening the door to economic development.

Rajiv Gandhi understood the prominent role computers were playing overseas and he was determined to loosen the regulations that had previously blocked India's fledgling IT companies from fully developing, instructing his aides to help out the nation's high-tech companies by finding international customers. The aides came back from the United States with a sweet present: a project for Wipro with GE—a big one. The company was off and running, and would make Azim Premji the richest man in India.

T. K. Rao—Texas Instruments

Rajiv also allowed something that his mother never would have: When an Indian living in the United States—T. K. Rao, an executive with Texas Instruments—requested in 1984 that the American company be allowed to set up in Bangalore at what's now called Electronics City, Rajiv gave it his nod. The arrival of Texas Instruments was more than a mere foreshadowing of the future: the company also used a private satellite that could beam information and phone calls from Electronics City to Dallas—a luxury at a time when overseas phone calls from India required prebooking an appointment with the operator (most available slots were inconveniently in the wee hours of the morning) and then putting up with a scratchy, warped connection that made it sound as if the client's voice were traveling from a far distant alien planet. Texas Instruments won many friends by offering use of their satellite to their Electronics City neighbors, overnight making communications of all sorts—data transfers, Internet, and phone—miraculously effective.

Sunil Bharti Mittal—Bharti Telecom

Sunil Bharti Mittal is another of those dynamic entrepreneurs whom I have personally known for a long time and admired while watching his rise firsthand. Starting as a small trader, he had the foresight to launch Bharti Airtel Limited and shepherd it to become one of India's leading telecommunications services providers, now with a market cap of over $30 billion, while he has become India's third richest person.

Mittal is another whose simplicity is disarming. When I was president of the Cellular Operators Association of India (COAI), Sunil and I pitched in together to help define the new policy of the government that would knock down the barriers that had been blocking widespread cell phone use. He was always very focused about what he wanted to achieve in telecommunications: to make his company the largest and most successful—as a matter of personal pride but also because he saw his role as providing a world-class communications service that would help boost the growth of the Indian economy.

As much as his ability to see around the bend, Mittal, a handsome legislator's son from a middle-class family of Punjab, bears a quality that has helped him make his name in business locally and globally. At a conference or some other occasion, if you chance to ask a question that impresses him, he will more than likely not only walk up to you afterward to hand you his business card, but will write you an e-mail an hour later saying he was so glad to have met you. Foreign reporters are stunned when they make inquiries that Mittal himself calls them back. Members of the media have often been dumbfounded that he's been able to deftly negotiate his way out of even the prickliest problems, working with competitors who are out to throttle him by insisting there is room for them all. Beyond a mesmerizing charisma, Mittal's down-to-earth manner that Indians love so much has helped him succeed from his earliest days, and the same qualities eventually won him foreign backers.

He started his business life humbly, in time accumulating a stash of cash—no small trick since his business up till then involved trading bike parts and generators. He then began lobbying the government about phones. He was dreaming of introducing a stunning innovation that India had not yet embraced: mobile phones. When the government liberalized the telecom sector in 1992, private companies began to move in, among them Bharti Airtel, which started its mobile services in Delhi in 1995.

But the network was bare-boned and the expense was exorbitant: A handset cost nearly a thousand dollars, and rates began at a painful thirty-five cents a minute. Mittal saw what was needed: a new network. Even though his company was at the time taking in only a total of $5 million in sales a year, Mittal was determined to set up a cell phone network using the GSM technology; for Delhi alone the cost would be $100 million. Despite the risks, he dived in, and succeeded.

As the industry grew, Mittal went on to play a pioneering role in bringing down tariffs progressively from thirty-five cents to two cents a minute, the lowest in the world. And suddenly, with millions of potential customers able to afford to connect via mobile phone, the industry blossomed. Hundreds of thousands of Indians began signing up every month. Today, Bharti Airtel has over thirty-five million subscribers and a market valuation of over $30 billion.

Mittal had his eyes on all sorts of new projects. Starting in 2004, with backing from the powerful Rothschilds of Europe, he was planting seeds for a revolutionary plan. He called the operation Field-Fresh Foods, initially aimed at bringing Indian fruits and vegetables to Europe. Along the way, the project is also renovating India's ailing food-delivery system, with plans ranging from cold-storage transport, to modern warehouses, to cargo planes, in a major push to boost food exports and simultaneously give farmers more money and needed incentive to update their methods. Starting by setting up a research lab and model farm—where farmers learned new methods to grow uniform, high-quality fresh produce that drew customers overseas—Mittal began contracting with several hundred farmers for fruits and vegetables. Over the next few years, he hopes to have thousands of acres to draw from for FieldFresh.

Meanwhile in 2006, Mittal announced a venture with Wal-Mart to introduce the chain to India, with at least some of the food products coming from Mittal's contracted farms. His partnership with

Wal-Mart for the venture in India is likely a step toward spreading his wings across many areas of business in many countries of the world.

Jehangir Ratanji Dadabhoy Tata— The Tata Group

It's a measure of the man and the life he lived that Jehangir Ratanji Dadabhoy Tata came to represent an exalted idea of Indianness: progressive, benevolent, ethical, and compassionate. JRD, as he was known by commoner and king, was another powerful man of Indian business who epitomized a way of life and a culture of business that cared, without thought of reward or riches, for his country and its people, a revered icon who considered his leadership of the Tata Group and his dedication to the cause of India as complementary. JRD brought to these undertakings a rare dignity and sense of purpose.

As a young man, JRD loved both France and flying; it was said of him that he spoke French better than English and both better than any Indian language. That did not preclude him from forging a special bond with people of his own country of all ages and backgrounds. Kalpana Chawla, the Indian-born astronaut who perished in the Columbia space shuttle disaster, cited JRD and his pioneering airmail flights as her inspiration for taking up aeronautics. He touched the lives of countless others, rich and poor, manager and worker, as he became the embodiment of the principles and philosophy of the House of Tata.

No one could have guessed how destiny would unfold when JRD was born, in Paris in 1904, to R. D. Tata and his French wife, Sooni. Educated in France, Japan, and England before being drafted into the French army for a mandatory one-year period, JRD later wanted to extend his military service to have a chance to attend a renowned horse-riding school. His father would have none of it. Leaving the

French army saved JRD's life, because shortly thereafter while on an expedition in Morocco, his regiment was wiped out.

JRD entered the family firm as an unpaid apprentice in 1925. The first of his adventures in business was born of his childhood fascination with flying, and he became one of the first Indians to be granted a commercial pilot's license. A year later a proposal landed at the Tata headquarters to start an airmail service. JRD needed no prompting.

In 1932 Tata Aviation Service, the forerunner to Tata Airlines and Air India, took to the skies. The first flight in the history of Indian aviation lifted off from Drigh Road in Karachi with JRD at the controls of a Piper Cub–like de Havilland single-engine aircraft. JRD nourished and nurtured his airline baby through to 1953, when the government of Jawaharlal Nehru nationalized Air India. It was a decision JRD fought against with all his heart, since the airline was never just a business for JRD; it was a labor of love. Tata executives would always be complaining—in private, undoubtedly—that their chairman spent more time worrying about the airline than he did running all of the Tata Group. JRD's fondness for and commitment to Air India was, while he was at the helm, what made it a world-class carrier.

Over JRD's fifty-odd years of stewardship, the Tata Group also expanded into chemicals, tea, automobiles, and information technology. Breaking with the Indian business practice of having members of one's own family run different operations, JRD brought in professionals and turned the operations into a business federation where entrepreneurial talent and expertise were encouraged to flower.

Conducting the affairs of a business empire as panoptic and complicated as that of the Tatas would in itself have been a prodigious task, but JRD had far more to offer. He played a critical role in increasing India's scientific, medical, and artistic quotient. The Tata

Institute of Fundamental Research, the Tata Memorial Hospital, the Tata Institute of Social Sciences, the National Institute of Advanced Sciences, and the National Centre for the Performing Arts, each an exemplar of excellence in its field, were projects that would not have come to fruition without JRD's steadfast support.

Kiran Mazumdar-Shaw—Biocon India

The rise to success is never easy, all the more true in India, and still more true if one happens to be an Indian woman. Just ask raven-haired Kiran Mazumdar-Shaw, who is always pictured with a very wide smile across her cherubic face. Her achievements are all the more surprising given the way her professional life began. After earning an honors degree in zoology from Bangalore University, Mazumdar-Shaw did graduate work in Melbourne, Australia, qualifying as—of all things—a master brewer, India's first woman in that profession. At first it looked as if she might make a career of it, following in the foot-steps of her master brewer father.

It was when Mazumdar-Shaw returned to her homeland—with the goal of becoming India's first female brewmaster—that the prob-lems began. Although she'd never encountered it in her modern household, there was an aura of forbiddenness about alcohol in gen-eral; the idea of a female concocting this liquid evil was simply shameful. Door after door shut in her face.

Mazumdar-Shaw returned to her first love, biology, but even there made little progress. The sciences were still a world mostly for men; while it might be tolerable to have a meek lab researcher spend her days in a back room quietly pondering amoebae, few wanted to contend with a self-confident female who had pioneering ideas for research.

For two years, Mazumdar-Shaw remained unemployed, almost jealous of her husband, who each day set off to work at his textile company; he continually offered to give her a job, and she continually turned it down. She finally set up her lab in her garage and began playing around with extracting enzymes from the papaya.

Finally one summer day in 1978 the phone rang. On the line was a representative of an Irish biochemical firm called Biocon that wanted to use enzymes in detergents and soaps. The outfit wanted to break into India—but they couldn't do business there as a foreign-owned firm. Would she be interested, they asked, in buying seventy percent and heading Biocon in India? So Mazumdar-Shaw headed to the banks, hearing the same sounds as she heard from the breweries, which is to say a succession of loud slams. When all else fails, you borrow from family and friends. Money in hand, she went about looking for a suitable place to set up her lab—only to hear the same slams. Landlords wouldn't rent to a woman; for that matter, she couldn't even find a secretary.

Temporarily forced back to her garage, Mazumdar-Shaw kept working. From papayas, she isolated an enzyme that could tenderize meat; tropical fish yielded a collagen that could clear cloudy beer. In short, there in a tiny ten-by-ten room, not far from the tire irons and bags of golf clubs, India's biotech industry was born. The next year, by which time Mazumdar-Shaw had found a bona fide laboratory and secretaries and lab workers, Biocon became the first Indian company to begin exporting enzymes, which were used to make paper, textiles, industrial catalysts, and to preserve food.

The biotech field kept growing into new areas, and offers began coming in from all corners, and Mazumdar-Shaw was soon accepting money from U.S. firms that were in awe of her work. By then she'd begun working with new ways to develop insulin—a pressing need in India, with over a quarter of all the world's diabetics. European pharmaceutical firms were swooping in as well to see what Mrs. Biocon, as she'd come to be known, was up to. Developing oral insulin, new cancer drugs, and trying to perfect vaccines to ward off cancer, Mazumdar-Shaw kept galloping into new frontiers—though the ride still wasn't smooth: the Irish owners had sold their thirty percent to another outfit, which tried to steer her research back to industry and away from health care. In 1998, Mazumdar-Shaw finally bought them out, but it didn't take long for labor disputes to roar up. After her technicians unionized, Mazumdar-Shaw drove to the lab one day to find them burning her effigy in the parking lot. She fired them all, fully automated the manufacturing unit, and kept galloping on.

When Biocon India went public in 2004, as the largest biotechnology firm in the country, Mazumdar-Shaw's personal holdings were said to be worth just shy of half a billion dollars, making her the wealthiest woman in India.

I could profile a hundred more Indian businesspeople whose stories resonate with messages of a country full of extraordinary talent and ability. But I think Indians today admire most of all those who send signals around the world of the new might of India's leading companies, a might that becomes so evident when the television channels and newspapers around the world feature stories with titles like "The Tata Group Acquires Britain's Corus Steel for $12.1 Billion." And then there's the previously mentioned acquisition of the U. S. firm of Novelis Incorporated, the world's leading producer of aluminum rolled products, for $6 billion by the AV Birla Group.

To proud Indians, stories like those say, Pay attention to us—India has arrived on the scene.

Looking Ahead

Lawrence Summers, the former president of Harvard University, said during his February 2006 visit to India that Harvard had made a "fundamental error of judgment" in not recognizing India's potential and promise early enough. A mistake, he said, that Harvard would correct soon by setting up a dedicated "India Center" with an initial funding of a billion dollars.

In April 2007, India's GDP crossed the watershed trillion dollar mark for the first time, and in terms of purchase power parity, India became the world's number three economic power. The prime minister noted that the continuing positive news has generated great global interest in India and also "has contributed to a renewed sense of optimism." The country has achieved its highest growth rate in eighteen years, matching Chinese levels and reaffirming widespread global talk of an "India story."

That story is beginning to be heard around the world (and I hope will spread all the more through this book). Case in point: A cover item in Britain's prestigious *Economist* trumpeted that "the Indian tiger is on the prowl . . . the roar from Delhi is echoing across Asia. After peevish years cast as China's underperforming neighbors, the huntress is now in hot pursuit." In a prediction that made every Indian businessperson smile, the article went on to say, "India should soon overtake Japan and become the third biggest economy, behind only America and China."

CHAPTER 3

A SLUMBERING
ELEPHANT
AWAKENS

Setting: Mumbai

India's most cosmopolitan city, Mumbai, sits on a claw of land that curls into the Arabian Sea from midway up the west coast. Once a string of seven mangrove-fringed fishing islands, now stitched together with causeways, this frenetic metropolis of thirteen million people, including movie stars, industrialists, financiers, and mobsters, holds most of the country's wealth—whether you're looking at capital assets or declared personal riches. Half the tax revenues of India wing from here to Delhi.

As the epicenter of India's banking, advertising, and media industries, Mumbai exudes a brazen showiness. It leads the pack in an increasing trend of blatant materialism, the likes of which have never been witnessed in India before.

Of all Indian cities, Mumbai is the place where you're most likely to rub elbows with the rich and famous. India's infamous film industry, Bollywood, has its base of operations here, though it can be hard to tell the difference between a film star and a wannabe—even the middle class are quick to flaunt their affluence. One reason they've been able to so prominently strut their stuff comes from recent decisions made by

Mumbai's banks, most notably the introduction of credit cards, which have triggered such a consumer spending spree that Western companies are now galloping into this market with dollar signs in their eyes.

In a country that until recently shunned money for money's sake, the top TV show became *Who Wants to Be a Millionaire*—or rather, India's spin-off of it, *Kaun Banega Crorepati*. Here, where "capitalist imperialism" was long scorned and foreign trade was shut out, the door flew open to the flashiest goods from abroad, which for decades could only be smuggled in: Swatch watches and Swarovski crystals, Ray-Bans and Versace, Louis Vuitton and Levi's, are now Mumbai's status symbols—and their widespread availability here has lightened the load for India's world travelers, used to hauling home suitcases of the brand-name treasures from overseas. India's six million luxury consumers are now furiously shucking out some $15 billion a year for diamond-encrusted watches, flashy cars, designer clothing, pricey cosmetics, perfumes, and high-tech gadgetry from digital cameras to Internet-connecting phones. Swarovski, for one, was so enthralled when sales doubled at its eleven stores in India during 2004 that it quickly opened nineteen more.

And in Mumbai—as the city has been officially known since 1995, when the nationalist local government cast off the name branded by Europeans (although Bombay still sticks; even locals occasionally refer to it by the old moniker)—the concept of "hot property" is an understatement in every sense of the word: this densely populated urban area spreads out over the most expensive land in the whole country.

Mumbai's treasures are so vast that they even register globally, with more homes valued at over $1 million than anywhere else in the world, including the minipalaces of half the thirty-seven Indians on the *Forbes* "World's Richest" list. Swanky palaces dot the waterfronts of the city's ritzier communities, home to some of the tens of thousands of India's

Mumbai has some of the most expensive real estate in the world—over eighteen million are packed around the cresent-shaped bay, with a density more than triple that of Tokyo.   (*Hindustan Times*)

multimillionaires. (Yes—tens of thousands of *multi*millionaires. It's still difficult for older citizens of this country, much less foreigners, to come to terms with just how many vastly rich people there are now in India.)

Locals claim you can find more Rolls-Royces, Ferraris, Mercedeses, Porsches, and Jaguars racing down Mumbai's streets (or at least trying to—usually impeded by an almost permanent wall of traffic) than anywhere else on the planet. Brimming with dazzling, space-age apartment towers that make many of America's fanciest condos seem downright ho-hum, and jammed with see-and-be-seen restaurants, Mumbai is the place where haute couture houses breathlessly compete for a place on the city's well-watched runways and where jazzy clubs lure jet-setters who party all night; the sea-hugging metropolis of hills tumbling down to the coast also spills gorgeous views from around nearly every bend.

Yet, just as a visit to Manhattan would not provide an accurate picture of how the rest of America lives, thriving, jiving Mumbai doesn't hold many clues to a view of the rest of India. But even if the realities of life are still uneven, are the changes that started in Electronics City and have fueled the consumer boom in Mumbai an indicator of growing prosperity throughout this vast, diverse land?

The short answer is: Yes, indeed.

The Rise of the Consuming Class

On the ground level, the boom in India's economy and its disposable incomes was triggered in the heart of the Mumbai financial and banking world. The expanding economy put more than a few dollars into the savings accounts of the average Indian: here is where the banking system spawned a revolution of its own, by extending billions of dollars in personal credit. They don't call it a retail loan or buying on credit; they call it the disarming, less threatening EMI, for "equal monthly installment." As a slew of foreign banks landed on Indian shores, both foreign and national players began vying for a larger share of the banking services pie, a market where retail loans by themselves are worth about $46 billion and headed northward. With Indian banks getting their act together and foreign banks raring to make their presence felt, the Indian consumer is being spoiled by choice.

In India, it's been said that "the only reason why American families don't own an elephant is that they have never been offered an elephant for a dollar down and easy weekly payments." And if the remarkable growth figures of the Indian banking sector spanning the last five years are any indication, one might be forced to believe that Indian families are no less comfortable taking on credit debt than are their American counterparts. The Indian consumer, because of colonial prejudices toward moneylenders, had always considered taboo the buying of a house or a car on loan. Now that attitude is being plowed under. The enthusiasm of Indians to consume as their disposable incomes continue to rise, and their enthusiasm for taking out a loan to pay for everything from a television set to a trip abroad, is making bankers happy. Whether it's a good thing for the Indian family is an open question.

But it's good for the banks, a fact that's come to the attention of bankers around the world, leading more and more foreign banks to steer business toward India and even to buy stakes in Indian banks. The list of foreign banks lined up to join the money parade includes global stalwarts like Deutsche Bank and Citigroup, and investment banks like Goldman Sachs, JM Morgan Stanley, and Barclays. Merrill Lynch has heeded the call and upped its ownership share in an Indian operation from forty percent to ninety percent.

One early player was the Industrial Credit and Investment Corporation of India, now familiarly known by its initials, ICICI. "We realized there was a huge opportunity," says Rajiv Sabharwal, senior general manager in the bank's retail liabilities department. "Income levels were rising, while the government was lowering the personal tax rate," and meanwhile more people were working, including many young. It all led to more disposable income—and ICICI wanted to tap it. In 1999, the bank began opening up thousands of new branches across the country, including in small towns, where the only limited banking services for decades had been in the post office.

ICICI also introduced automated teller machines, previously unknown in India. "A lot of people were dubious—they said we were crazy," recalls Sabharwal. "They said Indians would be baffled by the technology, that everybody would be afraid to use these new machines." But by

2000, most cash withdrawals from ICICI branches were being handed out of ATMs—and other banks dashed into the cash machine scene, introducing thousands more of their own. According to Euronet Services India director of sales, P. M. Srinivas Rao, the number of ATMs in India is poised to grow from the existing 25,000 to 250,000 in the next five years. "It's a forty-percent annual growth," he estimates.

Then ICICI did the unthinkable in this credit-wary land: They began offering millions of charge cards as well as loans to buy houses and cars. Kaboom! "Previous customers were averse to any kind of credit," Sabharwal recalls. ICICI almost single-handedly changed that. Hoping to tap the new middle class and the under-thirty-five worker, the bank threw the net wider while making the application process easier. Despite India's inherent shyness of taking credit as recently as a decade ago, plastic is ruling today. And what started with a small consumer base in urban India has now fanned out to other cities as well.

Once a nation of savers who stashed rupees away for a lifetime—hiding their savings in cash, gold, or even diamonds—today's Indian, even in rural areas, has been bitten by the consumption bug, thanks largely to the increased disposable income in the hands of the great Indian middle class, a segment of society virtually nonexistent until the middle of the last century. Estimates vary, with some putting the number of middle-class Indians in 2005—households with incomes between ten thousand and fifty thousand dollars—as high as the three hundred million figure noted earlier.

With the government now setting aside billions of dollars for roads, electricity, and telecommunications to develop rural India, the next economic boom and consumer splurge will be coming to the villages and smaller towns.

Indeed, after one study recently trumpeted the fact that the rural population—home to seventy-four percent of the population—was responsible for over half of consumer spending in India, the long-ignored countryside turned into a tantalizing gold mine. Everybody from soft-drink vendors to mobile cataract clinics (!) began stamp-ing out to the hinterlands and beckoning villagers to buy, even when the company had to hire a bicycle rickshaw to get the goods there or offer their products in miniversions—a tiny bottle of shampoo, or as-pirin sold two at a time.

Microfinance—loaning small sums to enable the poor or disen-franchised to start a little business—has been changing the face of rural industry as well. It has a proud history in South Asia; I might even say that "one of our boys made it": Bangladeshi Muhammad Yunus received the Nobel Prize for his pioneering work in this field. Yes Bank has also gotten into the microfinancing business and has joined forces with a number of organizations, in particular to open the door to women entrepreneurs. Expanding on the original micro-financing concept, Yes Bank is extending loans to women for projects from developing biotech to creating new types of textiles, which has resulted in major social and economic changes for their communities. And, along with other banks, Yes Bank is tapping the rural market, loaning millions to farmers to upgrade farming techniques, and set-ting up experimental "agri parks" with backing from retail market chains—allowing farmers to rent plots and knowing they have a guarantee of an outlet for their crops.

Banks, too, have been flocking into the villages—opening up new branches and sending "banks on wheels" to far-flung areas. Some new village banking kiosks have computers that employ fingerprints or iris scans instead of ID codes, simplifying the process for people not yet up to speed on push-button operations while at the same time making the process more secure. As their operations increase, bankers are dis-covering that not all rural villages are dirt-poor: some savvy farmers are heavily playing the stock markets. Defying expectations and logic, more diamonds, televisions, and Mercedes-Benzes—and gold—are sold in rural areas than anywhere else in India.

As the middle class grows, the loudest ka-ching in the organized retail market is by far fashion—not surprising, given Indians' adoration of splendid garb. Out of every $10 a family spends, Indians hand over $4.80 for clothes, shoes, accessories, and textiles for saris—nearly three times as much as they do on food and groceries. And India's young are leading the way. According to Technopak, "they are spending on books, movies, music, cell phones, food, and brand-name clothes." Levi Strauss recently saw revenues triple, and Benetton saw a sixty-percent jump in annual sales during 2005 alone. It's one reason the chain is adding another fifty exclusive stores to its more than four dozen existing outlets.

That stampede to the market marks the most earth-shaking change in India over the past three decades, says billionaire banker Uday Kotak. The new millennium, he says, is empowering today's generation and unleashing a new mind-set apart from the "general euphoria that accompanies a booming economy." The main factors behind this change are the rapid rise in the numbers of female workers, who now account for some eighteen percent of the workforce, and the rise in the service industry, which is employing millions of young Indians at wages rarely seen before, leaving them with large disposable incomes—especially so for the many who continue living with their families even after marriage. And the effects are explosive: India is now going from being a nation of savers to being a nation of spenders.

This reversal marked a revolutionary ground-shift, resulting in a remake of Indian culture, where the emphasis has always been on save, save, save. Traditionally, a workingman bought gold with whatever he could scrimp from the family budget, and when he retired, he spent the savings to buy a house, which he and his wife, his children, the grandparents, and maybe some aunts and uncles, along with some of their children, all moved into. That's what Indians always did—until rising incomes, credit, and a newfound optimism, mixed in with slick advertising and product placement, began prompting them, particularly the young, to open their wallets.

By 2005, Indians were collectively spending over $375 billion on personal consumption annually—and that ring of the cash register is being heard around the world, particularly since it grows louder each year. With the average Indian worker's wages shooting up a dazzling fourteen percent annually, Indians are purchasing nearly everything in mouth-dropping numbers: lipsticks and skin-whitening creams, washing machines and Reeboks.

Retail: Starting to Roar

Retail, the largest industry in the world, is coming to Indian shores in a big way. The chief executive (Delhi) of operations for Reliance Retail, Navneet Saluja, was very upbeat in a recent private conversation. "In India," he said, "retail will be the next revolution, bigger than even the telecom one." But what's coming will be a dramatic change for India—which, at twelve million, already has the highest number of retail outlets in the world. For the most part, though, these are small outfits that typically rake in only about two dollars a day.

Driven by changing lifestyles, strong income growth, increased use of credit, and favorable demographic patterns, organized retail in India is expected to grow at a blistering twenty-five percent annually. Yet the current small outlets—kirana stores, offering a minimal selection of fruits, vegetables, and household necessities like soap—are tremendously personalized. The owners know their customers by first name and have insights into their needs and finances. They provide extensive credit and home delivery, and go out of their way to meet each customer's personalized needs. Even taking in so little cash each day, the full family lends a hand, including the children—and with that much unsalaried help, the family can afford to keep the store open whenever there's business to be done. At lunchtime, the wife takes over; after school, it's the children's turn. In cases of dire need, they'll open the store even at night to serve their customers, who are also neighbors and friends.

These practices may soon be more the exception than the rule, however. The family-owned corner store, even the famous labyrinthine farmer's markets, are suddenly competing with sprawling supermarkets and one-stop "hypermarkets" introducing to the Indian palate previously impossible-to-find food items, such as factory-made yogurt, preground flour, breakfast cereal, and fresh basil and thyme. There is no one icon more symbolic of the change sweeping across the country than the arrival of the glittering multistoried shopping mall, where every weekend millions of eager spenders congregate to eat, dance at discos, and shop.

The concept of the mall is still relatively novel in India's hinterlands. And whenever you go to one you can expect to experience walking gridlock on the escalator as hesitant first-timers—mostly adult—try to muster the courage to step on the moving stairs. As recently as 1995, India was a mall-less land. The once-fabled, now old-fashioned souks and spice bazaars are becoming part of the culture's historical mystique while architecturally sleek and air-conditioned shopping arcades multiply. In 2000, India had a dozen malls; by 2006, there were over 150, and at least 350 malls will have shot up by the end of 2007.

The Media Impetus

Today's parade to the malls and brightly lit new retail stores is certainly being sparked by messages crafted in Mumbai, home to most of India's TV networks. And that, too, is new: until 1991, India had only a single network, state-run, staid, and commercial-free. The 350 plus channels now beaming into some sixty-one million homes via satellite and cable are thick with advertisements for fast food and colas, cars, jeans, and credit cards—all implanting a new sense of Western-style materialism in Indians.

Given the Indian people's apparently insatiable appetite for filmed musical melodramas, Bollywood has had a major impact on national attitudes and beliefs. Previously these films for many decades kept the Indian moviegoer on a steady diet of socialist-tinged morality films where the hero—perhaps a rickshaw puller, a farmer, or a coolie—battled factory owners and the landed rich, whose dripping opulence was unmistakably villainous; the heroes usually ended up as poor as they started, but at least they landed in the arms of the virtuous gal of their dreams, whose sumptuous form was glimpsed only when the lovers frolicked in the rain or splashed around under a waterfall. But just as movie venues have changed—air-conditioned multiplexes are replacing the tiny mom-and-pop theaters where the whirring of the fan competed with the volume of the flickery film—so have the plots.

Materialism is no longer taboo. The Indian filmgoer today gets an eyeful of hot cars, designer brands, and stylish hairdos, not to mention the sexy hip-jerking of scantily clad beauties. Modern Bollywood's hero has ditched the rickshaw, raggedy clothes, and anticapitalist stance. Instead, clad in Tommy Hilfiger and Armani, he drives a Porsche or Maserati, flashes a wallet bulging with bills, and prowls clubs where Western rap music blares, as he flirts up mini-clad babes and sips on a cola drink. And the drink is likely to be a form of advertising in a style borrowed from Hollywood: in a new wave of "product placement," the manufacturer has paid handsomely to have his product up on the big screen. For a film industry that was until recently facing a huge cash crunch, the extra source of rupees is more than welcome.

Bollywood stars, idolized by the millions, are the powerful brand ambassadors for consumer products, helping to spur the consumerism that is overtaking the country. Peering down from billboards, smiling from magazines, and enticing from television ads, the country's actors are paid millions to promote products from cookies to face cream to automobiles and insurance.

The reigning queen of the Bollywood sale-athon is Aishwarya Rai (unfortunately no relation of the author). Lovely and talented, a demigoddess for many, a former Miss World, she is in real life a very warm person—too warm, say conservatives who objected to her on-film kiss, in a country where suggestive movements are okay but kissing is strictly taboo. Seen by American viewers on Oprah and Letterman around the time her full-lipped pout was captured on the cover of *Time*, she's "Asia's most beautiful woman." Ash, as she's known to fans—some of whom worship her in shrines—wrings as much money from her off-studio moments as from her work in front of the camera. Her delicate wrists belong to Longines, the Swiss luxury watchmaker, her tapered fingers have been leased to De Beers as backdrop for diamond sparklers set in Indian-made Nakshatra rings. Her skin, once touched by Lux soap, now is claimed to glow from Lancôme.

If Kiran Mazumdar-Shaw of Biocon has become a symbol of what a woman can achieve in the New India, a forward-thinking lass named Ekta Kapoor is doing the same for the country's youth. With

The beautiful Aishwarya Rai   (*Hindustan Times*)

a family background rooted in live theater, Ms. Kapoor has created the country's largest and most successful media production company virtually from scratch. Since producing her first blockbuster television program at nineteen, Kapoor has rewritten the script on television entertainment for the masses. She has created more than twenty soaps on ten major Indian networks, plus a comedy series with a five-year run. The Indian showbiz industry watches her every move, with older, more experienced producers quick to copy any new Kapoor concept. This young wizard of Indian television is quoted as saying, "The rich do not need values, the poor do not have time for them. It's middle-class values that my serials are about."

As creative director of Balaji Telefilms in Mumbai, Kapoor, now thirty-two, continues to produce absorbing dramas that consistently strike a chord with viewers across the subcontinent. Kapoor is notorious for her eccentric habit of picking names for all of her television productions that start with her "lucky" letter *K*. When I shared the platform with her for the launch of one of her new youth serials sponsored by our foundation, she was jovial, witty, and surprised me by confessing that she prefers to stay in the background rather than deal with the glare of public scrutiny.

Word of Kapoor's amazing business alchemy eventually reached media mogul Rupert Murdoch, who arranged for his company, Star Group, to purchase a twenty-five-percent stake in her burgeoning business.

The Auto Sector Revs Up

In 1947, a young man named Brijmohan Lall was uprooted by the partition of India and Pakistan described later in the next chapter, arriving in India with nothing but a small bag and big dreams. He strode into a newly opened Indian heritage school and registered himself for classes. At the time, he was all of six years old.

After finishing school, Lall set up a small company to provide poor people with bicycles. The family's success mirrored the nation's steady growth through the next three decades as they continued making bicycles while pioneering a concept virtually unknown in India: fair treatment of the factory workers. Lall is now head of a world-respected company, the Hero Group—the world's largest producer of motorbikes and two-wheelers. Today his daily schedule as chairman of Hero Honda—the result of a savvy joint venture with the Japanese automaker—is beyond merely busy. He tells me with confidence that India will indeed become the most competitive automobile and auto-parts producer in the world in the coming decade.

Lall belongs to an industry that perhaps more than any other reflects the rising prosperity of the Indian worker. In 1995, 250,000 cars were sold in India; in 2006, the number rose to 1.1 million. Add to that the fact that the rickety pre–Cold War Indian-made cars and clumsy Ambassadors are now being replaced by the sleek Porsches and muscular Endeavors. A dozen major automakers, led by General Motors, Ford, Mercedes, and Porsche, are all vying to grab a slice of the booming India auto market. Industry experts foresee a global car market in which only two countries offer major growth potential: India and China.

But the presence of these global auto makers on Indian roads is just the tip of the iceberg. India's finance minister showed more than just a little finesse in his budget proposal for 2005–06 by offering big excise breaks for small-car purchases. That gave major car companies the push they needed to firm up their plans for India to become the small-car hub for Asia and Europe, earmarking billions of dollars to set up manufacturing plants throughout the country. India's two major advantages are the lower cost of production because of lower labor costs, and the world-class quality of India's engineering and design workers.

Telecommunications Gains Speed

The telecom sector is one of the better examples of the rise of India as an economic powerhouse in the twenty-first century. The mobile phone market in the country has emerged as the fastest growing in the world. During the later half of 2006 India was adding nearly seven million mobile subscribers *every month*—surpassing even China's explosive cell phone growth.

Market valuations of the telecom companies have shot through the roof. Along with Nokia, others like Motorola, Sony Ericsson, LG, and Samsung are involved in a brutal battle for a market that sees Indians buying more than a hundred million handsets yearly. With telecom infrastructure being put in place in the farthest reaches of the country, there is little doubt that the almost fairytale-like success story of the Indian telecom sector will continue.

The astounding success of the telecom sector can be traced back to the astute practical policies of the government in reducing licensing fees and encouraging competition. Currently the rates in India are the lowest in the world: all India calls from anywhere to anywhere cost two cents a minute, in the city less than a cent a minute. And telecom companies no longer rely on telephone calls to generate revenue. Messaging and other value-added services ranging from music and news downloads to e-mail now account for more than ten percent of revenues, and this share is bound to increase as the culture begins to depend on the mobile phone's full range of communication tools.

The projected growth of the mobile phone market brings to mind the old line, "the sky is the limit." According to one government spokesman, "We will achieve 250 million phones by 2007 and 500 million phones in five years and—who knows—one billion phones soon after."

Rockin' Real Estate

The real estate story is another jaw-dropper. In these last five years alone, I've personally witnessed land and property prices going up anywhere from a minimum of a hundred percent to as high as a thousand to fifteen hundred percent in some areas. My own sons walked away from buying a piece of land on the Delhi–Jaipur highway in 2003 because the price was too high, only to see it go up by a factor of ten within three years. The real estate megaboom can be heard everywhere, from large cities to small towns, to villages, and even in remote, previously inaccessible agricultural regions. Developers and investors lap up anything they can lay their hands on. They will tell you that anyone with a proper title to his/her land has to beat prospective buyers away from the door with a stick.

The source of the upward price pressure isn't hard to figure out: five hundred million people in rural and urban India still require good housing. Add the twenty million future home owners born every year and the unending demand becomes clear.

As I mentioned earlier, the residential real estate market exploded when credit made buying apartments and homes within reach of almost every earning household so that young couples suddenly did not have to wait like their parents did. More and more of those in their twenties and thirties are now moving out of their parents' house into condos and homes of their own, kicking off what amounts to a social revolution and the first widespread appearance of the Indian nuclear family.

The Manufacturing Crunch

Almost all industry talk about the rise of India in the twenty-first century revolves around the incredible success story of the IT and the IT-enables services sectors. Most analysts, including many in American think tanks, seem to suggest that India will emerge as the back office of the world while China will remain the low-cost factory. This belief has prompted many to suggest that the foundations of

India's success story are shaky because the country is not in a position to compete effectively with China in manufacturing.

Look at the case of Tata Steel, written off in the 1990s as a relic of the socialist era, destined for the Indian version of Chapter 11. In fact, when cheap steel imports were allowed after 1991, it did appear as if Tata Steel—saddled with obsolete technology, aging machinery, and a huge workforce that could not be removed because of Indian labor laws—was headed for difficult times. Repressive laws and regulations had ensured that the Tata Group, arguably one of the most respected corporate houses in India, did not have a large enough war chest to shore up its defenses against global competition.

Yet Tata Steel has emerged as a classic case of the revival and resurgence of manufacturing in India. After going through years of painful restructuring during the 1990s, the company has earned the title of one of the lowest-cost and most competitive steel producers in the world. For three successive years since 2003, the prestigious American Steel Institute has been rating Tata Steel as the best steel company of the year, better performing than giants like Nippon, Mittal, Arcelor, and POSCO.

Tata Steel's purchase of Corus group, mentioned earlier, marked a watershed in Indian corporate history. Ratan Tata, the heir who now runs the Tata Group, said, "When we first talked about acquiring Corus, many thought it was an audacious move for an Indian company to make a bid for a European steel company much larger than itself. That was something which had not happened before." The purchase makes Tata the fifth largest and the lowest-cost producer of steel globally, called by one banker "the coming of age of India Inc. in the global arena."

Other examples of Indian manufacturing can be seen throughout the country. Moser Baer has emerged as the largest manufacturer of computer storage devices such as compact discs in the world. Essel Packaging is the second largest manufacturer of packaging material. Arvind Mills is a world leader in the weaving of denim. Bharat Forge is the world's second largest producer of forgings for world auto-makers.

In a revealing article, "Coming Home to India," *Financial Express* wrote that "India is where global businesses are turning, to train their CEOs for tougher battles." This is where the action is, and India is no more a punishment posting.

So the question isn't whether India has lost out in the race for manufacturing, but how India can illustrate its strengths to the rest of the world.

A Taxing Quandary

In the same way that banks are encouraging Indians to invest in the formal banking sector, the government is trying to lure businesses out of the shadows. Though times are changing and new lower taxes are encouraging many to bring their money into accountable assets, the hard truth is that as much as fifty percent of India's economy still operates under the table. The process will take time but one thing is for certain: The money, even when hidden from view, is being put to excellent use by smart traders and businessmen. And it's money that does help accelerate growth.

In fact, it's precisely the issue of higher taxes that helped create the underground economy to begin with. Prior to the 1990s, tax rates were sky high—about eighty percent—and many Indians, not surprisingly, hid their income and their riches; much of that money secretly went into gold and the building of homes and office space for self-use. This was a nasty little cat-and-mouse game that everyone played and no one talked about. Foreign trips to the United States or Europe, or the purchase of quality diamonds, or the throwing of lavish parties or stays in hotels, were more likely than not done using unaccounted money. The tax man would look the other way—for a "fee," of course. The government didn't collect anything like the tax money that everyone would have been paying if the rates had been pegged at a reasonable level.

Now the tax system has been restructured in a flat rate that maxes out at thirty-four percent. Many of those hidden transactions came out into the open and the government even collected taxes on a lot of previously hidden accumulated money and assets—helped by an amnesty with the promise of no criminal penalties and lenient arrangements to pay back taxes over a period of time for those who had been covering up their income for decades. Tax collections have swelled; in the first nine months of financial year 2006–2007, corporate tax collections increased by over fifty percent. Customs duty on imports, which had been as high as three hundred percent, have now been brought down to a maximum of ten percent.

Although some still pay little or no income taxes, India is waking up to its role as a leader among the world's countries and is coming around to more sensible tax laws—and compliance.

Doing Business in India: A Few Tips

In the last ten years and more, a great many foreign companies—including no small number of major U.S. firms—have landed on India's shores. Many have met with reassuring, even glorious, success; others have packed up in the night and quietly slipped away. While of course there is no set of rules that guarantees success, my observations of this parade of winners and losers have led me to a set of dos and don'ts that may be useful.

First and perhaps most important, don't expect that an established, respected, even beloved brand name will buy you any success in India. A good example is Kellogg's. The cereal king barreled onto the Indian food market in 1994, confident that Indians, like the Chinese some time earlier, would be bowled over by their world-famous breakfast flakes. Despite the near universal name recognition, plus the power of a lavish ad campaign trumpeting that Kellogg's vitamin-fortified products helped battle anemia, sales figures fell miserably short of their goals: Kellogg's could barely scoop up even twenty percent of their initial target for corn flakes.

The problem wasn't simply that Kellogg's cereal cost three times more than locally made cereals. Even more important was that Indians prefer their breakfasts hot—and trying to satisfy that desire by pouring heated milk on the cold cereal resulted in a runny bowl of milk-sogged mush. Sales started poorly and plummeted from there, until Kellogg's got wise and developed an entire line of hot cereals appropriate to the tastes of this new market.

Although Kellogg's has more than quadrupled the demand for breakfast cereal since—Indians were eating over five tons of it by 2001—sales for their products are still marginal. The company introduced Cheez-Its in 2002, only to yank them the next year along with assorted cookies; even cereals geared specifically to India—such as Mazza, a product with a mango or coconut taste—have failed abysmally.

Kraft was aware of the cross-cultural marketing sinkhole. They couldn't stir up much enthusiasm over their faux orange drink Tang, officially launched in India in 2001. Initially, Kraft was determined: the company even set up a new factory in Hyderabad and trotted out new lemon and mango flavors, before abruptly putting the last lid on their Indian powdered-breakfast-drink experiment two years later.

Surprisingly, in this Hindu-dominant country, where four out of five refuse to even think about eating the holy cow, McDonald's— cautiously launched in Mumbai in 2001—has not fizzled out: the company has nearly a hundred outlets and announced in 2006 that it would open a hundred more. The reason sounds like the answer to Wendy's advertisement, "where's the beef?" You won't find it under the golden arches here. For India, McDonald's uniquely developed a noncow menu—including McMaharajas, made of lamb. Given the high percentage of vegetarians in India—some one in five—the fast food chain underscored its commitment to the market with separated vegetarian and carnivore kitchens: those on the side making McMaharajas can't even cross to the veg side (where workers wear green aprons and fry up spicy McVeggie and potato-laden McAloo Tikki) unless they first take a shower. While McDonald's India was slightly splattered in the 2002 fallout over beef-based flavoring used in fries (even Ronald McDonald was defiled during protests in Mumbai), the company has still done remarkably well—with sales shooting up some fifty percent a year.

In short, the critical rule in India is, "know thy market." But even those who study Indian consumer habits inside and out, who don't overestimate the importance of their name, and don't overlook "swadeshi"—the Indian traditional loyalty to buying local first, a concept that goes back to the time of Gandhi—still need a dose of good luck. "Destiny," we call it. Those who do overcome the obstacles and research the markets thoroughly can do extremely well and can tap into a gold mine that gleams more brightly each year.

As India increasingly becomes an innovator of technology, foreign firms are recognizing the leg up they can get by having enough managers and executives on the scene to spot tipping-point ideas early. A good way to learn the Indian market is to make sure that some of your staff is posted here. "By sending their key personnel to India, a lot of international companies get a chance to blend the experience from established markets with the enthusiasm of the Indian personnel," says Matthew Banks, senior VP at Integreon, the New York–based research and consulting company. "By moving the senior management to Bangalore, we're looking at taking an early advantage of the inflection points in technology and industry," adds Wim Elfrink, chief globalization officer for Cisco, the IT and communications giant.

One thing is for sure: India is a virtual gold mine of treasure and buying power, if properly tapped and addressed. Indians have trillions of dollars' worth of savings—wrapped up in property, livestock, sparkling jewels, and precious metals—and are hoarding some $200 billion worth of gold. And banks, which hold only some $400 billion in the entire country's savings accounts, are going through elaborate schemes to get Indians to bring those savings to their institutions: some are now offering "virtual cash" for gold, against which they can make loans.

That's a rich mother lode, ready to be tapped by foreign companies prepared to understand the Indian mind and inimitable way of doing business.

CHAPTER 4

INDIA: SHAPED BY ITS HISTORY

No other country has lived with so complicated a past so equably, assimilating everything that has happened to it, obliterating naught, so that not even the intricate histories of European states have produced such a rich pattern as that bequeathed by the Mauryas, the Ashokas, the Pahlavas, the Guptas, the Chalykyas, the Hoysalas, the Pandyas, the Cholas, the Moguls, and the British—to identify a few of the people that have shaped India's inheritance.

—Geoffrey Moorhouse in *Om: An Indian Pilgrimage*

It's the 1850s and British engineers have fully embraced their brutal, self-proclaimed role as taskmasters over the sweat-drenched native workers who are literally moving mountains and laying track. This simultaneously inhuman and superhuman effort will eventually create a massive railway, part of a transportation system that will, for the first time, tie together the far-flung parts of what we now know as India. The native workmen are given orders to gather some old bricks that have been found lying around not far away, bring them to the site, and lay them to aid the construction of the rail system. Some sixty years later, a British visitor notices something special about the bricks; his observation triggers an excavation campaign at the site where the bricks were found.

Those bricks, so innocently used in the building of the railway, were the clue that led archaeologists to discover, at the Mohenjo-Daro site in the Indus Valley, the remains of an ancient civilization dating as far back as 2600 B.C.

A perfectly designed grid system served as the planning map for uniform streets, and a mile-long man-made canal easily gave traders and fishermen direct access to the sea. The diggers were stunned to discover that this ancient city boasted modern amenities. Every house was equipped with indoor well-drawn water and, incredibly, interior bathrooms—probably the planet's first. The community had sophisti-cated dockyards and advanced systems for irrigation and flood preven-tion. Archaeologists were further excited to find furnaces, water storage tanks, and grain warehouses, along with pottery wheels and kilns for metals; these ancient people had devised new metallurgical techniques, creating alloys and precise tools for measuring everything from weights to lengths to time. Clay figurines that realistically portrayed anatomy forced the experts to revise the "known facts" about early art.

Other works showed men practicing yoga, the first time the med-itative practice was recorded. The world was thunderstruck by an-other finding: the jaw of an Indus Valley man who had actually been to a dentist and had his tooth decay carefully drilled away.

Those traders, fishermen, and artisans who lived in the two-story brick abodes built around shady courtyards in cities such as Mohenjo-Daro were enjoying lifestyles and conveniences that historians had previously shrugged off as impossible for the times. The discovery of this ancient Indus Valley civilization flipped numerous assumptions about early human existence on their ears.

Today, elements of this early iconoclastic society still persist in contemporary Indian culture, which often appears out of sync with the rest of the world. This is a land of innovators: archaeological finds and translations of ancient texts are now causing the Western world to credit Indians with being the originators of everything from arithmetic to cosmetic surgery, which the Indus Valley people were performing centuries before the birth of Christ.

Invasions

The centuries immediately surrounding the birth of Christ were culturally rich for India, a blossoming in every arena during an era of peace and prosperity, with great leaps in science, astronomy, medicine, and metallurgy. In mathematics, the major advances included the concepts of zero and infinity. Even Albert Einstein acknowledged mankind's debt: "We owe a lot to the Indians, who taught us how to count, without which no worthwhile scientific discovery could have been made."

The period was also rich in poetry, literature, education, and architecture, as well as philosophy, sculpture, music, and painting—including the remarkable cave paintings of Ajanta. Tourists still flock to see the "rustless wonder" in Delhi—a single cast piece of pure iron that stands twenty-three feet high and weighs six tons. Made of ninety-eight-percent pure iron, it has never rusted—incredibly, since the methods of metallurgy that could achieve this purity or even melt the iron ore were lost for centuries afterward, testimony to the high level of smithing skills of the period.

India was the proverbial "Golden Bird," with rich reserves of everything from shimmering diamonds (some the size of walnuts), to valuable pearls, coral (the coveted red variety was used as hard currency), gold, and cotton, coupled with artistic skills that churned out embroidered brocades, dyed fabric in rare colors such as indigo (which only India then possessed). Caravans of elephants, camels, and oxen loaded with packs of textiles, spices for curries, jewels, sandalwood incense, and perfumes lumbered into Central Asia and plodded back loaded with silver and gold. Indians were trading in all directions—with the Javanese and Balinese, with Egyptians, Greeks, Syrians, and Romans.

Alexander the Great charged into the northwest area called Punjab in 327 B.C., encountering little resistance from the pacific natives. The subcontinent of that day was a disorganized mess, fragmented into kingdoms scattered across the land. The hundreds of rajas and chieftains only occasionally fought each other except over land, or sometimes for women, either as slaves or to expand a ruler's harem. But they never sought to unite against enemies. So when the mighty warriors of ancient Greece marched in, the locals might as well have rolled out the red (hand-stitched, of course) carpet. The failure to join forces against invaders was a security weakness that would strategically plague Indians for centuries to come.

Only one brave ruler, Porus, did stand up against Alexander, though Porus's war elephants and limited fighters were quickly outbattled by the Macedonian. But Alexander, in admiration for the bravery Porus had shown, spared his life. After roping the western territory into his empire, Alexander soon turned his army back toward the west, leaving behind Greek forces to hold the ground. Cartographers who traveled with Alexander were able to map out trade routes for European travel to India, and caravans soon followed in his chariot tracks, paving the way for India's destiny to unfold.

The long history of invasions that followed Alexander the Great—from Mahmud Ghazni's ruthless plunder of the Indian subcontinent in 1000 A.D., to Nadir Shah's invasions in 1739, to the colonization by the British—left many psychological scars, difficult to erase. One notorious example is the grim practice of sati, in which a widow is burned alive on the funeral pyre of her dead husband. Many historians agree that the practice never existed in ancient Hinduism and was first witnessed only around the tenth century, many Hindu women preferring suicide to being repeatedly raped and sold into harem slavery by Muslim invaders. As Hinduism turned increasingly inward under the onslaught of repeated and ferocious Muslim invasions that routinely destroyed temples, cities, and towns, this act of suicide became a rigid and pernicious practice that is unhappily still found today in pockets of India.

These first Muslim rulers, beginning with Muhammad Ghauri from Afghanistan in the twelfth century, unleashed a reign of terror on Hindus, massacring those who wouldn't convert and clearing the land of any other religions while trying to implant their nascent Islam, although their kingdoms usually didn't extend deep into the subcontinent. Even the more tolerant among these early rulers made life difficult by slapping non-Muslims with steep taxes known as jizya. The early-sixteenth-century reign of Ibrahim Lodhi was so brutal—he slaughtered even Muslims whom he didn't regard as devout enough—that some of his advisers sent an SOS to Kabul, then ruled by young Zahir ud din Muhammad Babur, a descendant of the Mongol warrior Genghis Khan, who had been trying to extend his new kingdom. Babur trudged into Delhi in 1526, lugging along a few cannons, and in a matter of hours his ten thousand warriors overthrew the Lodhi sultanate that had been entrenched in Delhi for nearly four decades—winning the enormous Koh-I-Noor diamond as just one of the war spoils. With this foothold, the planting of Islam in India began in earnest.

Babur's grandson, Akbar, who ruled in the late 1500s, came as close as a Muslim leader could to accepting Hinduism. Abolishing the exorbitant tax on non-Muslims, he was ultratolerant of all faiths, actually calling in Jesuit priests, Persian fire priests, and Buddhists monks for long discourses and going so far as to create his own home-brewed state religion that mixed Islam with Hinduism, Christianity,

Buddhism, and even a dash of the Persian Zoroastrianism. His rule is still considered to be one of the brightest eras of Indian history, when cultures blended and debates flourished.

Although often ruthless, the Mogul rulers also had a penchant for poetry and art. They brought in designers from Persia, adding an international flair to the cityscapes as stunning new architecture appeared across the land. Ornate tombs, onion domes and the slender minarets of new mosques, scalloped arches, lacy latticework, and splendid gardens became commonplace across the land.

The peace that Akbar brought did not last long after his death. Things turned radical once again during the reign of Shah Jahan's ruthless son Aurangzeb in the late 1600s. Shah Jahan had ruled over the greatest era of Mogul prosperity in India, though he is certainly best known for the magnificent Taj Mahal, which he commissioned as a mausoleum for his favorite wife, Mumtaz Mahal. Unfortunately, in 1658 he fell ill and was tossed in prison by Aurangzeb, who grabbed the throne and proceeded to kill all his brothers, along with most of his own sons—presumably out of fear that they would turn against their father as he had turned against his. A zealot, Aurangzeb obliterated all signs of other faiths, condemned Hindus to death unless they converted, and launched a jihad to forcefully yank unaffiliated kingdoms into his empire. His military campaigns, while successful, pretty much emptied the treasury.

Europeans, unable to resist the reports of riches and exotic spices and materials coming from the region, then joined the fray. The Portuguese sailor Vasco da Gama landed in India in 1498. His successful return, loaded down with exotic spices, can be tagged as the beginning of Western world trade. The Indian port city of Goa, then under the rule of a Muslim sultan, was soon captured by the Portuguese, who made it their most preferred trading post.

The Taj Mahal is generally considered the finest example of Mughal architecture. (*Hindustan Times*)

Shoving the sultan out, the Portuguese immediately began evangelizing—employing imaginatively vicious and cruel methods to convert the Hindus to Catholicism. One of the "state-of-the-art" persuasion procedures involved rubbing beef on the mouth of an uncooperative Hindu—rendering him, by his own religious scriptures, an untouchable for life; another was the public hacking off of limbs for religious crimes imagined or invented.

The invaders also set fire to hundreds of beautiful temples and serene shrines, and nailed Hindu priests to crosses; no Hindu names were allowed to be uttered, and Hindu festivals, weddings, and dress were made taboo. And when the sadistic Inquisition Board arrived in 1560, matters only got bloodier (if that were possible), as the Inquisition that the Portuguese unleashed in Goa was far more brutal than the notably nasty one going on in Europe.

Hindus, as well as any other non-Catholics—including Syrian Christians and a community of unfortunate Jews who'd come to Goa to escape Spain's Inquisition—were accused of heresy, many burned at the stake in grand bonfire festivals accompanied by the ringing of church bells. The roundups prompted a mass exodus of many non-Catholics from the region, fleeing terrors that continued unabated for the next three hundred years.

Despite the trail of carnage that followed them, the Portuguese adored the European-styled Goa they created—building lavish churches, quaint white chapels, a hospital, and even shipping over a printing press, Asia's first. They eventually gained several other territories, but Goa—the first European settlement in Asia—remained their headquarters, even after their foes the Dutch (who ultimately yanked much of the spice trade from the Portuguese) began routinely blockading the settlement in the mid-seventeenth century, cutting off trade for months at a time. Goa became a fashionable travel destination, a veritable Palm Beach, for wealthy Portuguese. In fact, the Portuguese so adored their private enclave that they wouldn't let go—not even when India finally gained independence in 1947. (It would require an invasion of the army of Prime Minister Nehru in 1961 to forcibly remove the Portuguese from Goa.)

And then, in 1612, the British fleet arrived and fought a vicious sea battle with the loathed Portuguese, a fiery show visible from Surat on the western coast. Their victory gained them the favor of Mogul ruler Jehangir, who soon granted the British rights for trading across the empire. The British set up their first warehouse in Surat and continued charming their way across the land, negotiating separate deals with the princes and chiefs in the south and the east whose kingdoms weren't ruled by the Moguls. Buying land along much of the coastline, and setting up major trade centers in southern Madras and on the east coast near Bengal, the center of the cotton trade, the British had established nearly two dozen posts by 1647. They also finagled ownership of Bombay, then a string of seven islands on the west coast that had been seized by the Portuguese. When the British king Charles II wed Portuguese princess Catherine of Braganza, he requested that Bombay be tossed in as part of the dowry, fortuitously giving the Brits another major stronghold on the Indian subcontinent.

In 1717, by which time the emasculated Mogul leadership was limping along and the British East India Company, which had been created in 1600 with the intention of obtaining trading privileges in India, was controlling larger and larger swatches of the region, the Brits convinced the Mogul ruler to drop any excise duties on goods sold to the British East India Company—giving England a distinct advantage over other Europeans. Not long thereafter, the British gained more power when a war victory gave them rights to collect taxes from several eastern states.

Hardly clean-nosed in their earlier trade endeavors, which were filled with manipulations, bribes, and slippery deals, the British took advantage of their new status by assuming even more of a political role, starting in territories around Bengal. Their methods for collecting land taxes were often violent. Between the taxes and the effective monopoly they'd been granted, the British were able to force the cloth makers to lower their prices, then demanded customized products that sold well in their market, such as the ornate prints of calico, which became the rage. Weavers who resisted the wages proposed by the British promptly had their thumbs cut off. On top of that, the British inflicted taxes directly on textile producers, taxes so severe that producers often ended up in debt to the British even *after* selling them goods.

British India

The powerful European countries had collectively proclaimed that it was their manifest destiny to bring Christianity and the white man's "superior" ways to less enlightened parts of the world. In 1858

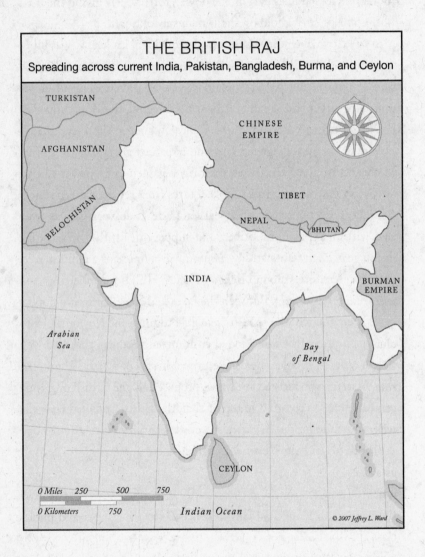

THE BRITISH RAJ

Spreading across current India, Pakistan, Bangladesh, Burma, and Ceylon

TURKISTAN

CHINESE
EMPIRE

AFGHANISTAN

BELOCHISTAN

TIBET

NEPAL

BHUTAN

INDIA

BURMAN
EMPIRE

Arabian
Sea

Bay
of Bengal

0 Miles　250　　500　　750

0 Kilometers　　750

Indian Ocean

CEYLON

© 2007 Jeffrey L. Ward

the British were pursuing that agenda when, after over one hundred and fifty years of occupation, they took over as self-proclaimed masters of the Indian people, marking the beginning of what's now known as the British Raj (the word is Hindi, for "rule").

For all its flaws, the Raj era did bestow some gifts upon India. The subcontinent had no effective transportation system; the Brits, needing efficient ways of bringing in goods for sale and shipping out raw materials, developed roads and a railway system across the country, which opened up routes between heretofore disparate territories. Infrastructure improvements such as the Bombay harbor and expanded irrigation systems were facilitated by the British Raj's self-serving motivations. Besides building roads and railways, the British connected the country by telegraph as well. They introduced an efficient postal system (again largely to serve their own commercial and military purposes) and in the year 1906 made Bangalore the first city in India to have electricity—used initially to power the British-run gold mines in Mysore.

British missionaries opened hospitals, orphanages, and schools, including universities—educating India's elite in the fine British tradition but teaching the masses with a curriculum that promoted the role of the slave. The British also took on a few admirable social causes—trying to prevent child marriages and infanticide of girls, as well as the funeral-fire practice of sati.

The British more than any other force led to the creation of India as a nation-state. But their finest gift to India—although it certainly wasn't considered such at the time by the Indians—was introducing the country to English, a language learned by the upper and middle classes, which would give India a marked advantage in the global market of the twenty-first century.

Beyond those laudable contributions, however, the British mostly dealt India a rotten hand, managing to kick a productive economy into the dark ages by crushing farmers with stiff taxes and blocking the export of Indian textiles and other products. The invaders plundered the treasury and made off with fine jewels—among them the Peacock Throne and the 105-carat Koh-I-Noor diamond, at one time the largest in the world (the name means "mountain of light"). The diamond now glitters in the queen of England's crown; India wants it back.

Although some British politicians supported out-and-out independence, others, such as Winston Churchill, believed the Indians didn't warrant even that. "India is a geographical term," he bellowed in a 1931 speech. "It is no more a united nation than the Equator." Churchill loathed India and all things Indian, didn't support independence, and downplayed the problems there—while the woes were growing daily. By 1932, even the maharajas had almost unanimously joined together in a call for India's independence. President Roosevelt leaned on Churchill to lighten up and grant freedom to the subcontinent. But still Britain was loath to cut India free.

Independence

All that changed in the late thirties as Hitler's soldiers goose-stepped down the Kurfürstendamm while war clouds gathered. England desperately needed the manpower and fighting skills of the British-trained Indian army. To India, the logic of the British demand contained a fatal flaw: Britain—declaring the need to fight Germany in the name of freedom—wanted India's help, but that same Britain was still saying no to freedom for India. In 1939, England simply announced that India had joined the war on the side of the Allies.

By 1941, Japanese fighters had taken Singapore and Malaysia, and had moved into a position to invade India. A desperate offer from Britain was put on the table: Sir Stafford Cripps arrived in 1942, promising independence if India got fully behind the war. More than two and a half million Indians would eventually serve in uniform, the largest all-volunteer military force in history—though the reason for many was less enthusiasm for the war effort than for regular meals, since the food supply for the mass of Indians was pathetically meager.

After the war, a reluctant England lived up to its agreement when the voice of Lord Mountbatten, then India's governor, crackled over the radio waves. The British crown, he announced, would grant India independence at midnight on August 14, 1947. The joy of the news was soon marred by an announcement from Muslim leader Ali Jinnah, a thin-faced man with prominent ears and an intense, intelligent look, who proclaimed that the plans under way for the liberation of India were "Hindu-dominated." Muslims would be relegated to second-class citizenry, he warned. At the news, riots broke out as Muslims attacked Hindus, killing thousands.

By June 3, Britain had modified the plan. India, announced Lord Mountbatten, was to be divided. The northwest of what had before been India and parts of Bengal in the east would be devoted to a new Muslim state, to be called Pakistan.

When the British finally quit the country, what they left behind in India was a picture of poverty and misery, a country with its social fabric on the verge of snapping. In the early eighteenth century when the British had started spreading their tentacles into the subcontinent, India, rich in resources and at peace with the world, accounted for an incredible twenty-five percent, more or less, of global trade; by the time the British boarded their ships in 1947, India accounted for no more than one percent of global trade. The British had treated the

Mohammad Ali Jinnah, an Indian Muslim politician and leader
of the All India Muslim League. He founded Pakistan and served
as its first governor-general.   (*Hindustan Times*)

people of India as servants, order takers, and second-class citizens of
their own country. They had created a mentality of "we're incompe-
tent, tell us what to do." The nation would have to find a way to regain its self-esteem and confidence.

But with the nation split in two, India as Hindu, Pakistan as Muslim, for a vast number of people independence wasn't exactly something to celebrate; it was time to pack up possessions and trek across
the new border to massive uncertainties. In what was the largest migration ever known, some fourteen million people switched places,
millions of Muslims heading west toward the land that would be
Pakistan, and even more Hindus heading east to India. Often hauling
little more than pots and pans on wobbly carts pulled by a starving
bullock, sobbing as they left their homes, many headed out on the

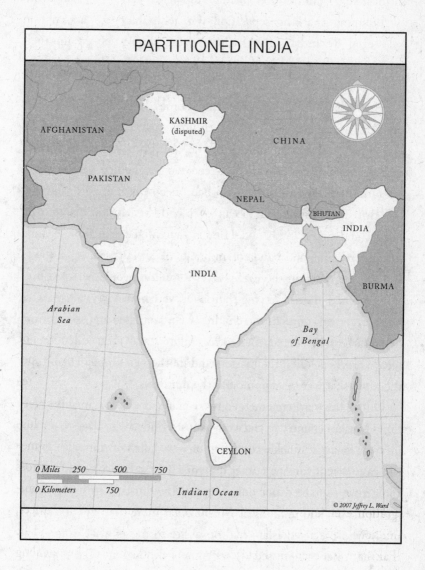

PARTITIONED INDIA

AFGHANISTAN

KASHMIR
(disputed)

CHINA

PAKISTAN

NEPAL

BHUTAN

INDIA

INDIA

*Arabian
Sea*

BURMA

*Bay
of Bengal*

CEYLON

0 Miles   250   500   750

0 Kilometers   750

Indian Ocean

© 2007 Jeffrey L. Ward

dusty road by foot; others jammed into trains so crowded that many suffocated; thousands more piled on top of the cars.

Assuming that the separation was temporary—an assumption held even by India's new leaders—some simply locked up their houses, believing they'd soon be back; many older Hindus, particularly in beautiful Lahore, did not want to leave, and their sons and daughters had to pull them from their homes. On horses, on oxen, on donkeys, on camels, and on foot, they came and they went, passing each other on the roads, all wearing the same grim expression of traumatized wartime refugees who'd seen too much. The partition and migration of these millions, who had once been unified in fighting the British, unleashed an ocean of blood, as Muslim slaughtered Hindu and Sikhs, Sikh and Hindus slaughtered Muslims, civilian battled civilian—and bands of militants of all faiths ravaged towns and the migrants on the roads. Over a million people perished over three months: trains carrying thousands were blown up; villages were set ablaze; men, women, and children were mutilated and strung from trees; fathers murdered their own children and then killed themselves; brothers killed their sisters and mothers to protect them from the rapes that were as common as the murders.

Out of the mayhem emerged two estranged siblings: an almost entirely Muslim country to the west—most Hindus who tried to remain in West Pakistan quickly converted or were killed or run out—and to the east, except for one corner designated East Pakistan, a shrunken India that contained not only Hindus, Buddhists, Christians, Jains, and Jews, but still millions of Muslims, far more than in Pakistan, as many who practiced Islam had no desire to move. That irony—one that the Americans missed almost entirely although it still eats away at many Hindus—was that Muslims cleaved the country in the demand that they have their own land, from which other religions were largely

About 14.5 million people crossed the border between Pakistan and India immediately after the Partition, hoping to find the relative safety of religious majority. (*Hindustan Times*)

excluded, yet so many Muslims stayed behind that India holds the second highest Muslim population in the world.

As inky darkness descended over Delhi on August 14, 1947, hundreds of thousands gathered at the city's Red Fort—the crenellated and bell-capped palace of Mogul emperor Shah Jahan. The keynote speaker, as head of the interim government, was dashing, sharp-featured Jawaharlal Nehru, who, like Gandhi, had spent nine years in prison, where he wrote three acclaimed books about British rule and the state of India, concluding that only revolutionary measures could fix the broken country. A brilliant orator, he took the podium and began to address the crowd in the clipped English that had become so ingrained during his college years in Britain at Trinity College in Cambridge, it was said he had lost much of his Hindi.

"Long years ago, we made a tryst with destiny," his voice boomed into the still night, "and now the time comes when we shall redeem our pledge, not wholly or in full measure, but very substantially. At the stroke of the midnight hour, when the world sleeps, India will awake to life and freedom. A moment comes, which comes but rarely in history, when we step out from the old to the new, when an age ends, and when the soul of a nation, long suppressed, finds utterance." As the twelfth chime of midnight echoed across the park, someone blew a conch shell—an ancient sign of victory—and the crowd broke into cheers and tears.

The separation and hard-won creation of the two independent countries was official. Conspicuously absent from the podium was Gandhi, the father of the nation; the night before, mobs had set fire to the small village where he lived with "untouchables"; angry and traumatized, he gave no independence speech.

Crisis

While the cheers of the Independence Day celebrations were still ringing in the air, India's new leader as prime minister, Nehru, had no time to catch his breath. In the split-up, the independent and tranquil kingdom of Kashmir had chosen to become part of India even though the vast majority of its population was Muslim. Threaded with rivers and placid lakes, laced with gliding white lotus blooms, Kashmir is cradled amid the dramatic folds of the ice-capped Himalayas, the world's highest mountain range, whose name means "home of snow." The alpine beauty of this remote Utah-sized region—where stately groves of pine stand over deep ravines, leopards prowl amid boulders, and painted canoes slice the glass-topped waters against a stunning backdrop of powdered peaks—has for centuries elicited comparisons with heaven. "If there is a paradise on earth," exclaimed Mogul emperor Jehangir in the seventeenth century, "this is it, oh, this is it." The region's decision to join India in the split was a thorn in the side of the Pakistanis. Just after independence, Pakistani armies crossed the border in an attempt to reclaim Kashmir.

Meanwhile the United States, eager to spy on the Russians and Chinese at the dawn of Cold War cloak-and-dagger politics, offered a friendly hand to Pakistan, which shared common borders with both Communist Russia and a China in the throes of a civil war that threatened to turn it into a companion giant Communist state (which would in fact happen two years later). In exchange for the United States receiving permission to set up a major military base in Pakistan, Washington agreed to support the Pakistani position in United Nations for a plebiscite on Kashmir.

This left India's Nehru in a panic. How could he prevent the beloved Kashmir from being wrenched away from India? He chose the only course he could perceive, rushing off to Moscow and committing to a deal that would prove to be an unholy alliance. The Soviets used their veto power in the Security Council several times in the following years to insure that India kept Kashmir. But India was to pay a heavy price, very nearly bringing the country to the brink of ruin.

For the next thirty years, until the 1980s, India marched to the Kremlin's tune in an era now labeled as India's "Soviet Tilt." Moscow effectively stifled the Indian economy; factories turning out everything from light bulbs to mousetraps to car tires were arbitrarily told by inept bureaucrats how many units they would be allowed to produce. The economy collapsed and a social structure that had served for thousands of years fell further apart.

Adopting a Russian-style centralized decision-making bureaucracy, the government required businessmen to beg and cajole for licenses to run their own factories. If you had to sneeze, the joke went, you had to ask for government permission. The government grabbed control of the banks and basic industries like mining and the airlines. Everyday food products and necessities for daily living—practically everything, in fact—fell into short supply.

Still, many businessmen managed to thrive by learning to adapt to the system. I was one of those who embraced the insanity to survive. My family had a steel business and a very small operation building selenium rectifiers, electronic components that preceded the transistor. I had just returned from the United States, a specialist in semiconductors with a graduate degree, so I was given the selenium rectifier business to run. The company was selling about $100,000 worth of product a year but had a negative worth . . . and was losing money. If anyone had told me at the time that I would eventually build that operation into a business with a net worth of $2 billion, I would have laughed at them.

At the time, transistors were just beginning to come into use, and I had learned enough to be able to manufacture them—though whether I would be able to sell any was another story. I lined up to apply to the government for a license to manufacture transistors. The government official appointed to review my application was a typical bureaucrat with some generic bachelor of arts degree and had not a clue about what a transistor was. But of course he had to pretend to be knowledgeable and an expert in the field. He told me his analysis showed that there was no market for as many as I was asking to make and that my application was being rejected.

My father, who is a healthy eighty-two now and lives with me, had even then, as the head of our family business, forewarned me about how this game had to be played. I meekly asked the bureaucrat how many he thought the marketplace needed. He came back at me with a completely arbitrary number. For fifteen minutes we bargained back and forth as if we were playing some kind of parlor game. Finally we settled on a number. I was satisfied, and he had played out his assigned role as a dedicated bureaucrat.

Over time, we learned how to play the game more efficiently. Need a license to import some raw materials for manufacturing? Ask for three times what you needed. Enterprise and the spirit of "never say die" were still very much part of the Indian psyche and made our will to face challenges even stronger.

Change Partners and Dance

To the Indian people's good fortune, several factors combined to bring an end to the appalling era of the Soviet Tilt. During the 1960s, young Indians of the upper class had gone abroad to be educated at Oxford or Cambridge, returning home with leftist ideals that matched the temper of the times. By the 1980s a further shift began taking place, with an ever-increasing number of Indian students heading to the United States.

As an entire generation of the Indian elite became more exposed to the Western way of life, that influence started seeping into the Indian middle class. Gradually, the ruling elite attained a firm grasp on the American perspective and were less enamored by the unfulfilled promises of Marxist ideals. For this new generation of young people, improving standards of living was more important than ideology, and it was clear that capitalism was getting the job done faster and more efficiently than the Soviet system.

Surprisingly, even the entertainment industry played a key role in changing the mind-set of Indians. During the 1980s, middle-class India fell in love with color television and there was an explosion in the sale of videocassette recorders. Suddenly, many more Indians were getting exposed to the "soft power" of America, delivered through Hollywood movies and music videos.

Until that time, generations of Indians had been brought up to believe that the austere lifestyle was right and good and that it was sinful to crave anything as superficial as consumer goods. That changed in the 1980s as consumerism gradually became a more acceptable social norm. This newfound affinity toward the United States brought ideas of open markets and a free economy, and resulted in a clamoring by India's businessmen to remove the shackles of the restrictive licensing and control laws.

Red No More

The collapse of the Soviet Union in 1991 carried an unmistakable message that all wisdom does not lie in the hands of the centralized government. At the same time, Indians began paying attention to the spectacular growth of the "East Asian Tigers"—South Korea, Malaysia, Indonesia, Thailand, and Taiwan. All had forged close ties with the United States and opened up their economies for global trade and capital flows. The results were dazzling. Until the late 1960s, all these countries had per capita incomes that were less than India's. By the 1980s, they had raced ahead of India.

But it was the major foreign exchange crisis in 1991, when India's foreign exchange reserves went so low that it had just enough dollars to buy a month's critical imports, that woke the country up to the realities of a commercial world and free-economy benefits. Pushed into a corner, the Indian government started a desperate, last-minute search for a massive loan to shore up the economy and avoid financial disaster and likely widespread starvation. The only one stepping up to the line to help was the old nemesis: Britain. The Bank of England would provide India with working capital, but only on the condition that India pledge its gold—a commitment that meant India would have to turn over a portion of its gold reserves if it could not repay the loan. Saving money in the form of gold was a fixed tradition in India; gold was, and still is, considered a matter of family and national pride. But India had no choice. Though the deal was signed, it was seen by Indians as a national disgrace.

It was the last straw, the final piece of evidence that the Soviet approach to running an economy was a disastrous failure. India's finance minister immediately opened up the economy to foreign investments, freed business and trade of all controls, and allowed businesses a virtual free hand to grow. The effect was nothing short of miraculous.

Rabindra Nath Tagore, the Nobel-laureate poet, writer, philosopher, and thought-architect of modern India, rightly envisioned almost a hundred years ago that it is only when India rises to her true greatness—including all its people and excluding none—that "the History of India will come to an end, merged in the History of the World which will [then] begin." As Tagore exhorts us to consider India's history as part of the greater history of the rest of the world, he unwittingly articulates the most ancient of Indian ideas: "Vasudeva Kutumbakam," or the world as one big family—through which India can accomplish what has been called "the spiritualization of the human race."

Perspective

No person who visits India would ever return with just one set of adjectives to describe the country and her people. India's long and convoluted history—at the same time tragic and majestic—also defies simplistic description. Despite its complexity, in order to understand India and its potential for the future, you must see clearly where it has come from. This whirlwind tour, amounting to a fleeting glimpse of thousands of years of history, will hopefully render a vision of India's colorful and tragic past, which will in turn speak volumes about how the mind-set and systems of this incredibly diverse, ancient yet progressive country exists and flourishes in our world today. Here is a country launching itself into a bright and new millennium, desperately shaking off the ghosts of dysfunctional mental slavery and abject poverty to be seen by the world as having at last returned to the glories of its earlier days.

The history of India is largely a chronicle of ten consecutive centuries of foreign invasions and long occupations. Though the Moguls, Portuguese, and British have all sought to capture India's riches and resources, India herself has never invaded a foreign land. Despite the incessant barrage of attacks, invasions, and cruelty perpetrated by imperial rule, people of virtually all major religions have settled here and integrated, without resistance, into the fabric of Indian society. From plundering its riches to converting Hindus through torture, from using divide-and-conquer tactics to destroying the liberal Indian psyche by creating a slave-and-servant mentality, the foreigners largely used and abused Indian hospitality.

Yet India harbors neither rancor nor revenge. Why? Indologist and Sanskrit scholar Max Müller has produced historical evidence to suggest that Hindus, in general, are "less prompted to vengeance for wrongs inflicted than any people on the face of earth," instead being "most eager for knowledge and improvement."

While the essential Hindu ethos of respecting diversity and revering truth gives Indians the courage to make contact with many cultures, this drive to be rid of the pains of the past allows a Hindu to make fresh beginnings with a light mind and loving heart. More than making money, this is the Indian's real joy: perfecting his role in the world, by raising his personal spiritual high-jump to greater and greater heights. It should come as no surprise, then, that this ancient spiritual tradition and philosophical heritage is just as alive today as it was millennia ago.

As testimony to India's peaceful and accepting historical nature, the world's widest array of belief systems live and function peacefully side by side. Today, though predominantly Hindu, beside having the second largest population of Muslims in the world (with more Muslims than in Pakistan), India is also home to over fifty million Christians (more than those in Italy or France), millions of Buddhists, Jains, conclaves of Israeli migrants who have never faced any form of anti-Semitism here, and the largest population in the world of Zoroastrians (also known as Parsees). This diverse and peaceful coexistence can be found nowhere else in the world, with the possible exception of the United States.

India's history is also that of our world, for how can one talk about India without referring to all the races that have touched her, loved her, conquered her, or violated her in some way? India has always been greater than just "India," pregnant with a past and a future at every moment in her history.

CHAPTER 5

FRIENDS AND TIGERS

The United States, India,
and China

As the blue-and-white 747 emblazoned with the words UNITED STATES OF AMERICA lifted off from the runway of Andrews Air Force Base outside Washington, D.C., in February 2006, President George W. Bush could wave good-bye for a few days to the steaming cauldron of discontent bubbling down below. Carrying the commander-in-chief, first lady, Secretary of State Condoleezza Rice, National Security Advisor Stephen Hadley, swarms of Secret Service agents, and a squadron of reporters, *Air Force One* climbed higher and higher, and turned in the direction of Delhi.

The president would escape for a few days from the criticisms ricocheting across the country over the tragedy of the war in Iraq that seemed to have no solution, and the grousing over oil prices skyrocketing toward seventy-five dollars per barrel.

Instead President Bush could revel in the news that of the sixteen countries covered in the most recent *Pew Global Attitudes Report*, India, where he would soon be landing, held a higher opinion of the United States than any of the others in the study. More than seventy-one percent of Indians had warm feelings toward the United States, for varied reasons, a chief one having to do with nuclear energy— long a source of friction between the two countries. Suddenly, thanks to President Bush, nuclear energy had transformed into a reason to further bolster the budding U.S.-India friendship.

The first glimmer of what was now unfolding between India and the United States—and would shape the global power structure in the process—had been evident eleven months before in Moscow. At a summit of world leaders in May 2005, President Bush brushed past the other heads of state mingling at a Kremlin reception, marching across the room to greet India's recently elected prime minister, Manmohan Singh. Introducing the first lady to the economist PM, and gushing about India's peaceful mix of religions and the country's growing energy needs, Bush laid his cards right on the table, announcing, "You and I need to talk civilian nukes."

Alas, there was a very big snag in that dream: Selling U.S. nuclear technology to India was prohibited, as it had been for nearly three decades. That prohibition was but one factor in the bitterness that for decades had defined relations between Uncle Sam and Mother India, a bitterness President Bush was trying to sweeten. He'd started a few years before, lifting sanctions on certain types of arms sales to India as an enticement for Delhi to sign up for his war on terror.

The U.S. sale of defensive radar systems to India in 2002 marked the first arms shipment between the two in nearly forty years. Not only did Bush brush aside arms embargoes put in place years earlier, he also granted military loans to India. The government in New Delhi was upgrading India's arsenal, and now had a long list of military wants—from fighter planes to advanced missile systems—although many purchases awaited final approval from the U.S. Defense Department, which appeared as surprised as everyone else by the new twist. "Only a few years ago," said the DoD in a press release, "no one would have talked about the prospects for a major U.S.-India defense deal [but] today the prospects are promising, whether in the realm of combat aircraft, helicopters, maritime patrol aircraft, or naval vessels."

In addition, the United States was forging a revolutionary strategic military alliance with India, complete with official agreements, defense advisory councils, and military exercises—on the ground, in the skies, and particularly at sea, where American and Indian ships jointly prowled the Indian Ocean, ensuring the sea lanes crucial for oil tankers were kept open. Officially aimed at battling terrorism, the military marriage of these nations raised eyebrows worldwide—and governments and think tanks from Australia to Canada commissioned investigative reports into the bilateral romance.

The China Target

Pakistan, long America's favored country on the subcontinent, was panicked that her worst foe was arming up and she was essentially being ditched after not proving terribly helpful in the war on terror or in the search for Osama bin Laden. But Islamabad was not alone in feeling deep dismay. China, estranged from India since 1962, was also rattled by this strategic coupling—and with good reason.

While Delhi and D.C. officially denied it, analysts said the union ultimately had Beijing in its sights. A Pentagon-commissioned report titled *The Indo-U.S. Military Relationship: Expectations and Perceptions,* by a Virginia-based think tank, the Information Assurance Technology Analysis Center, had been released in 2002. It drew on interviews with America's top military brass to conclude, "As the U.S. military engages India . . . we cannot separate our thinking on India from our thinking on China. We want a friend in 2020 that will be capable of assisting the U.S. military to deal with a Chinese threat. We cannot deny that India will create a countervailing force to China."

Simon Long, the South Asia bureau chief of *The Economist*, in a private conversation with me, said essentially that the rise of China makes it even clearer that India is the more natural strategic partner for America, and that it is not already so is a peculiar legacy of the Cold War. The process of unwinding those old suspicions and antagonisms was already well under way in the second Clinton and early Bush administrations, though it had a major setback after 9/11, which threw America into Pakistan's arms yet again. "In the long run," Long said, "a democratic, resurgent, modern, and responsible India will be the most dependable partner for the United States, and serve both their economic and military needs."

Meanwhile, China—seeing numerous reports about a strategic encirclement that included not just India, but South Korea and Japan—issued statements saying that such bilateral engagements as the Indo-U.S. arrangement "should not be directed against a third country." Clearly, Beijing was worried.

Whether it's actually part of a strategy to create a new Cold War against China, as some speculate, or a means to battle Asian terrorism and piracy, the U.S. government isn't officially saying. But it's just the latest unexpected turn in the bizarre relationship between two countries that, despite common bonds—expressed in the old saw about the United States being the oldest democracy, India being the biggest—has been tainted by suspicion and shredded by rivalries. For the past sixty years, the relationship between India and the United States has been defined by exactly what shapes it today: nuclear energy, military alliances, and arms sales. It's just that, until recently, those very factors usually marred the potential for friendship.

Many in the presidential party traveling to India that day must have been aware of the irony of the visit from a historical perspective. More than thirty years earlier, another Republican, President Richard Nixon, had traveled to China and stitched up a deal that effectively began the end of the Soviet Union as a strategic threat to the United States and simultaneously opened up a whole new world for American corporations. Some of the more optimistic members of the Bush team were no doubt hoping that history would repeat itself during this trip. A strategic alliance with India would not only strengthen the Bush Doctrine of spreading democracy across the world, but also help the United States contain the growing menace of terrorism.

For half a century, the story of relations between the United States and India had been a sad tale of unfulfilled potential. Despite being the two largest functional democracies in the world and despite myriad reasons for being allies, the two nations had remained more than just indifferent—they were actually suspicious and hostile toward each other.

Columbus and the Indians

In the past, India and the United States shared the common heritage of both having suffered domination by the British, who stifled exports of finished goods, hit both with excessive taxes, and tried to battle both into submission when they expressed desire to escape from the crown. But the odd bond between India and the United States began long before that—going back to Christopher Columbus. Sailing off with good intentions and bad assumptions, Columbus had set forth determined to find India (and Indonesia). When he made landfall, he was certain he had found the mysterious and elusive Indies. His insistence even to his dying day that the Caribbean islands where he had actually landed were in fact the Indies, and so the inhabitants should be called Indians, created confusion so vast and enduring that we still suffer from it, two hundred years later.

Once the location had been straightened out and stories of the exotic land swept the globe, India and her culture became an obsession—in nineteenth century America particularly, when every year hundreds of ships plied the waters between Calcutta and the East Coast; so frequently did treasures from South Asia arrive that Boston Harbor had a landing aptly named India Wharf.

Those early traders and sailors brought more than indigo dyes, jute, and the newly popular rubber; they arrived bearing more than painted tins of Darjeeling tea and hot spices, or chests heaped with tapestries, fine silks, and the softest cashmere shawls. Like Marco Polo centuries before, these American voyagers also carried books of ancient texts, jewel-encrusted swords, and stories of the turbaned traders on camels; they spread tales of fakirs who could lie on beds of nails, swamis who could levitate, and royal processions of elephants swathed in gems.

American enterprises began heading east: the Delano family (they would later couple with the Roosevelts and produce the four-term president FDR) made a fortune from shipping, hauling British-made opium from east India to China. Standard Oil sailed to the subcontinent and set up in 1882, hawking cans of kerosene as well as the glass hurricane lamps that burned it; a person's wealth, it was said, could be known by the number of lanterns illuminating the pathway to his door. Even financial institutions came. Citibank, then called the International Banking Corporation, opened in Calcutta in 1902, the same year that General Electric built India's first hydroelectric power plant to power the British-owned gold mines in the south.

By the early twentieth century, best-selling novels such as E. M. Forster's *A Passage to India* imprinted savory images of this faraway land, as did fine-art books that were pored over in posh salons, where hand-colored maps glorified British India. Super-rich Americans spilled out of ocean liners that docked in New York, their trunks filled with superb ivory carvings and intricate tapestries.

A less starry-eyed but equally startling picture of India began to emerge in the 1920s, as American reporters—not as heavily censored by the Raj as had the British and Indian press—documented the unsettling changes and upheaval of a country in the throes of a freedom struggle led by the great visionary Gandhi, with his call for freedom through nonviolent means, teamed with Jawaharlal Nehru, the Cambridge-educated lawyer who would be the country's first prime minister.

The U.S. government and the Congress backed India's call for freedom, though by and large the American people paid little attention to the goings-on in this part of the world, until independence was finally wrung from the British amid the massive blood-curdling carnage of Partition, sowing the seeds of unending friction between India and Pakistan.

Independence did, however, let Nehru bring India center stage as a responsible global leader, championing the cause of third world alliance, free of domination by either the United States or the Soviet Union. Despite his official alliance to the USSR, Nehru positioned himself as a diplomatic third party, often negotiating between conflicting views on the world stage. The Cold War, however, did not allow many to see him in such subtle shades of gray. In 1949, Nehru paid a state visit to the United States. President Truman greeted Nehru

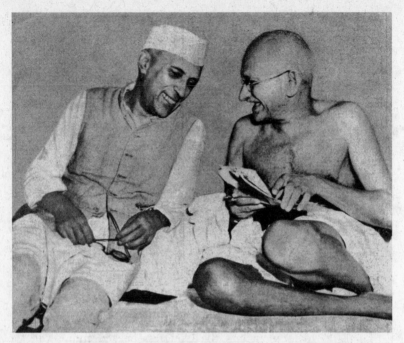

Nehru visiting with his great friend and advisor, Mahatma Gandhi
(*Hindustan Times*)

enthusiastically, while inwardly remaining suspicious—later telling a visitor to the Oval Office, "I can smell these Communists a mile away. And this man Nehru sure looks like a Communist to me."

Unfortunately, the American president's inherent (and misplaced) distrust of Nehru stood in the way of warming up the ties between the two countries. Cold War compulsions and a stubborn refusal to see and understand each other's points of view had destroyed any hopes of an enduring friendship between the two. It is a cruel irony of the Cold War era's geopolitics that a democratic India tilted toward the authoritarian Soviet Union, while military-ruled Pakistan was allied with a democratic United States.

Of False Hopes and Missed Opportunities

When Nehru's daughter Indira took over the Indian premiership two years after his death in 1964, Indo-U.S. relations took a further nosedive. Domestically, Indira Gandhi picked up where Nehru had left off, further tightening the government's hold on industry—nationalizing banks and forcing foreign companies to either go into partnership with an Indian firm or quit the country. Among the victims: Coca-Cola, which fled when faced with the prospect of their coveted secret formula falling into the hands of an Indian partner-company.

In 1965, the annual monsoons didn't come, and the next year the country was hit with another drought. The result was impending famine. India desperately went looking outside its borders for food. Their erstwhile partners, the Soviets, with not enough wheat to feed their own people, were in no position to help, leaving Delhi to go hat in hand knocking on doors in Washington. The Johnson administration, seizing the opportunity, was happy to help—but not without strings: The Indian government was to stop criticizing the U.S. role in Vietnam, open her fertilizer market to U.S. exports, and also devalue her currency. Even then the food aid was given on a very tight leash—Johnson ensured that India received only a month's supplies at a time to ensure her continued compliance.

In the long run, the aftermath of India's famine led to a benefit: Driven to make major improvements in agriculture, India embraced the so-called Green Revolution and eventually became self-sufficient in food production. Had it not been for the humiliatingly tight leash on which the food aid was given by the United States, the episode could have ultimately led to a rapprochement in Indo-U.S. ties. Many experts term it a lost opportunity.

New Delhi was further riled when in 1971 Henry Kissinger secretly visited China and toasted to Indo-China friendship. By then, the war between India and Pakistan over East Pakistan (now Bangladesh) had also begun, and the United States stood up in support of Pakistan—with plans to use the Islamic state "as a conduit in conducting secret negotiations with China." Reports suggest that the American Seventh Fleet would surely have attacked India during the war, had it not been for Soviet pressure, which stated that "any attack on India will be considered an attack on the USSR." This coziness with archrival USSR was taken in the United States as further evidence of India's Communist leanings.

During Jimmy Carter's presidency, a short glimmer of hope sparked to life a new beginning in Indo-U.S. relations. The hanging of deposed Pakistani prime minister Zulfiqar Bhutto by military dictator Muhammad Zia-ul-Haq in 1978 compelled the U.S. administration to suspend aid to Pakistan and impose sanctions while calling for a restoration of democracy in the country. There were hopes that India might change its pro-Soviet policy and work toward a rapprochement with America. But the hope died a quick death two years later, when the Soviet Union invaded Afghanistan and the Carter Doctrine was promulgated, which among other things enlisted Pakistan's help and offered it $3.2 billion in military and economic aid over five years. This further fueled Indian insecurity.

During the early 1980s, a series of meetings established a reasonable rapport between Indira Gandhi and Ronald Reagan. But it continued to be a zero-sum game, showing no signs of budging from the established U.S.-India and U.S.-Pakistan relations. The status quo remained: If U.S. cooperation with New Delhi increased, Islamabad would get upset . . . and vice versa. Despite these limitations, Reagan took steps to shift the Indo-U.S. relationship from conflict to cooperation. In October 1984, he signed National Security Directive 147, which promoted high-technology sales to India. But suspicions still existed between the countries—with India closer to the USSR while the United States sided with China and Pakistan.

Indira Gandhi's sudden assassination in 1984 and the stepping in of her young son Rajiv Gandhi as prime minister led to a major reversal of India's socialist policies, and Rajiv Ghandi moved toward making India a modern West-oriented nation. While on the one hand, his open capitalist-oriented policies infused fresh and young blood into the sagging fortunes of an otherwise state-controlled, low-growth economy, they also led to his defeat in the 1989 general elections, and under new leadership, the country slid further into socioeconomic disasters. By 1991, India was on the verge of economic bankruptcy and famine, leading to the Bank of England loan detailed earlier.

For years India had nervously watched the United States sell military weapons to neighbor and archenemy Pakistan. Determined to provide a balance for its own defense, India set out to develop an arsenal powerful enough to be seen as a deterrent, leading to a shock around the world in May 1998 when India conducted the first in a series of tests of nuclear weapons. An alarmed Clinton administration imposed sanctions against India. But logic prevailed: having a new member of the nuclear club as an ally made a great deal more sense than continuing a relationship of suspicion and mistrust.

High-level U.S./India talks began, initially between U.S. deputy secretary of state Strobe Talbott and Indian external affairs minister Jaswant Singh, with the purpose of bringing India in line with the U.S. nonproliferation goal. Yet as the talks continued over the years, the wider agenda of Indo-U.S. relations came into focus, eventually leading to a deeper understanding of each other's problems and bringing the two nations closer than they had been in twenty years.

Soon after, in May 1999, India and Pakistan landed in another face-off in the Kargil district in Kashmir. Pakistani soldiers and Kashmiri militants infiltrated the Indian side of the Line of Control (LOC), which divides the two nations. The Indian army and air force launched an aggressive counterattack, and Washington joined in vigorously pressuring Pakistan to withdraw its forces. The American support further thawed relations between Washington and Delhi.

In 2000, President Bill Clinton's highly successful five-day visit to India and Prime Minister Vajpayee's more subdued but successful visit to the United States signaled a new chapter in relations. Before Clinton departed Delhi, the two sides issued a joint proclamation that heralded "a day of new beginnings" and called for frequent summits, annual foreign policy meetings, and discussions about security and how to battle terrorism.

But the bulk of the proclamation, the very foundation of the new alliance, was pitched on commerce, investment, and trade. In a radical departure from the Nehru era, the Delhi government announced that it was hoping to boost foreign direct investment in India by at least $10 billion.

The year also marked yet another significant change: India's leading trade partner became the United States, far surpassing Russia for the first time in decades, as many of the richest and most powerful American businesses woke up to the new opportunities in India. But the warming relations turned chilly again after 9/11: India, having dealt with terror for decades, expected that an America desperate for friends in its new war on terror would come calling. Instead the United States turned to Pakistan, where many of the Taliban who had been waging the war in Afghanistan had taken refuge. From the perspective in

Delhi, Washington had once again failed to see the advantages of allying with India.

Support from Washington—Finally!

Despite supposedly joining hands with the United States in the fight against terrorism, India continued to suffer terrorist attacks that appeared clearly sponsored by Pakistan—including an assault on the Indian Parliament in December 2001 and an assassination the following May that killed Abdul Ghani Lone, one of Kashmir's most moderate leaders. When India threatened to respond with military retaliation against Pakistan, Washington stepped in, extracting a promise from Pakistani president Pervez Musharraf to stop infiltration across the LOC.

But the attacks continued, leading many in India to wonder how the United States was willing to bomb Taliban strongholds in Afghanistan but would not do the same when the insurgents slipped across the border into Pakistan. Despite that, Delhi waited patiently for America to see reason, and the Indian establishment "was careful not to align India with outspoken critics [of the war on terror] such as France, Germany, and Russia."

The restraint shown by Delhi in not criticizing America's intervention in Iraq, coupled with India's rapid economic growth, brought about a grudging consensus in Washington that India was fast emerging as a sensible, stable pan-Asian political and economic power. When U.S. ambassador to India David Mulford spoke at a Boston University alumni reception in New Delhi, he observed that "both of our nations have suffered at the hands of terrorists and recognize the necessity of eliminating this inhuman threat to our people."

Delhi's patience paid off. U.S. think tanks began to issue reports heralding India as a friend too long ignored. One study, sponsored by the Asia Society and the prestigious Council on Foreign Relations, said that India, "with its billion plus population, democratic institutions and values, steadily growing economy, and substantial defense equipment, represents a partner of great value" for the United States.

So when *Air Force One* carrying George Bush and his team landed in Delhi early in 2006, Bush had his task cut out. With his mind set on resolving all past hurdles and suspicions marring Indo-U.S. relations and a zeal to tap into the rising potential of India, Bush was prepared to offer the most historic deal ever with the Indian establishment: an agreement that would accept and support India as a nuclear nation that could help maintain a peaceable balance of power throughout the region.

A Nuclear Deal for India

When I met U.S. undersecretary of state Nicholas Burns during his visit to India in December 2006, on the eve of the signing of the U.S.-India civilian nuclear deal, he described the move as a significant strategic leap forward for the U.S. and Indian governments and their people, adding that the decision had strong support of both Democrats and Republicans. He also said that the United States and India had the ultimate unfulfilled relationship, which had been waiting for decades to be realized.

In many ways, the nuclear deal between the United States and India was quite unprecedented. Though details of the terms will be argued by pundits on both sides for years to come, the United States recognized India as a legitimate nuclear power and allowed India to keep a stockpile of deterrent nuclear weapons. The "bomb" part of

India's nuclear energy plans will remain a preserve of India and will not be open to inspections by nonproliferation teams of the International Atomic Energy Agency. India will, however, place the much larger and more substantive civilian nuclear energy plan on the table for negotiations as well as inspections and verifications. All nuclear plants in India generating power will be under the international safeguards, and the country will have to follow safety and nonproliferation requirements of the international agency.

Supporters of the deal—the majority in both countries—argued that detractors were naïve in comparing India with rogue states like Iran and North Korea and unstable allies like Pakistan. While there have been repeated signals and accusations that China and Pakistan have indulged in proliferation of nuclear technology, no one has ever doubted India's unflinching commitment to safeguard the technology.

The nuclear deal helped the policy establishment in India decisively move away from the Cold War–era suspicion and mistrust of Uncle Sam's intentions in Pakistan. It has made India very confident of its role as a major emerging global power, and one can sense this confidence in the mood of not just the top politicians and bureaucrats but in the common man too.

The Chinese Threat

Beyond the shared democratic history, the threat of Islamic terrorism, and the economic benefits to both nations, one of the most crucial factors driving the United States and India together is the growing economic and military clout of an increasingly aggressive and belligerent China.

As a report from the conservative Heritage Foundation described

it, "A close bilateral U.S.-India relationship supports a mutually beneficial insurance policy against [China's emergence as a threatening
regional and global power]—an insurance policy that conservatives
have every reason to welcome." Unless India can emerge as a credible
nuclear-armed counterweight, China could soon be threatening American interests in the Asia/Pacific region.

Not everyone agrees with this reasoning. Geoffrey Pyatt, the
deputy chief of mission with the U.S. Embassy in India, speaking
privately, said that it would be too simplistic and an old-fashioned
cloak-and-dragger approach to look at America's growing partnership with India as a "counterbalance to the growing threat of China."
In his view, "India and China are two large, powerful countries economically and one cannot imagine the USA playing any kind of a
chess game, balancing one with the other. America is looking at fur-
thering its relationship with both in mutually satisfying ways."

But consider for a moment the following rather nightmarish but
not inconceivable scenario of some time in the not-too-distant future:

- China, having become a major economic and military power, begins flexing its muscles in Asia and Europe, while the European
  Union, having become reliant on goods from China, caters more
  to Chinese diplomacy and maneuvering than to U.S. interests.

- U.S. multinationals, heavily dependent on their Chinese manufacturing bases and markets, begin lobbying for still more favorable
  treatment for China, despite the harm this may bring to the
  United States.

- The rise of the neo-left in Latin America—especially in
  Venezuela, Bolivia, and Brazil—and its close ties with the Chinese

regime becomes a strategic threat to the United States in its own backyard.

• China, having befriended totalitarian regimes in Africa and central Asia to secure energy supplies, moves to gain a stranglehold on these strategic reserves, posing a threat to the energy security of the United States as well as India.

If this scenario, or even parts of it, were ever to become a reality, the American unipolar world would be under a major threat. On India's side, the danger is of course more immediate, with the nation sharing not only a 2,175-mile-long, porous border with China, but also the historical baggage of animosity. What also troubles Delhi is the speed with which China is setting up naval and military facilities in Pakistan and Myanmar, close to the Indian homeland.

The twin swords of a possible Chinese domination on the one hand and rising Islamic extremism on the other have played a substantial role in bringing India and the United States together. Both nations have suffered at the hands of fundamentalist Islamic extremism. The case for Indo-U.S. cooperation in the wake of the rise of a Red China was brought out forcefully when President Bush affirmed via his September 2002 National Security Strategy that India and the United States, "the two largest democracies, committed to political freedom [and] protected by representative government . . . [have] a common interest in the free flow of commerce, including through the vital sea-lanes of the Indian Ocean . . . in fighting terrorism, and in creating a strategically stable Asia." In the same document it was also noted that a "quarter-century after beginning the process of shedding the worst features of the Communist legacy, China's leaders have not yet made the next series of fundamental choices about the character of their state. In pursuing advanced military capabilities that can threaten its neighbors in the Asia-Pacific region, China is following an outdated path that, in the end, will hamper its own pursuit of national greatness."

The U.S. Defense Department, the Pentagon, and sundry U.S.-based geopolitical think tanks have over the years expressed rising alarm over China's military buildup and expenditure, which has been growing at an annual double-digit rate since 1992. The Pentagon estimates that total defense-related expenditures were between $50 billion and $70 billion in 2004 and as high as $90 billion in 2005, placing China third in defense spending, after the United States and Russia. In response, China's latest military and strategic assessment, *National Defense in 2006,* claims that Chinese defense spending in 2006 was only about $36 billion. The Pentagon, of course, has always claimed that China's defense spending has been two to three times higher than China itself acknowledges. Independent U.S.-based think tanks estimate that Chinese military spending will grow to more than $200 billion over the next fifteen years.

Clearly uneasy about the emerging Indo-U.S. partnership in its vicinity, Beijing is already making overtures to sustain its preeminence in the region. One China watcher, Dr. Parama Sinha Palit, has written that "after Pakistan and Myanmar, Beijing is skillfully employing economic and military means to draw Bhutan, Bangladesh, Nepal, the Maldives, and Sri Lanka into its orbit," leading many in the American and Indian establishments to worry about a preeminent China causing security dilemmas in South Asia. By recognizing and empowering India as a major global player—through the civil nuclear deal or defense support—Washington hopes, in Dr. Palit's view, to "engage New Delhi as a 'hedge'" against the growing Beijing influence.

When a Nontransparent China Calls the Shots

It's also becoming apparent that the balance of global economic power is gradually shifting to Asia, especially China and India. Reproduced from the *Global 2020 Report*, a possible scenario of the year 2020 demonstrates that the impact of the growth in China and India over the next fifteen years could reshape the globalization process, giving it a more non-Western face.

This fear is spelled out in a report from a group under a member of the president's staff, the director of national intelligence; the report imagines a letter that might be written in the year 2020, from the head of the World Economic Forum on the eve of the annual Davos meeting. Warning of the impact of Chinese economic supremacy on the United States, this fictional letter says, "America is no longer quite the engine it used to be. Instead the markets are now oriented eastwards. . . . In the last few years, the whole balance, as I now realize, has been shifting. Asian consumers are setting the trends, and Western businesses have to respond if they want to grow. Fifteen years ago, few of us knew anything about Asian firms. Now we have Wumart. China also got Washington's attention when it started diversifying its foreign currency holdings and the U.S. public awakened to the fact that it had been living way beyond its means. . . . I'm reminded that businesses, if one thinks back to the East India Company's total rule over the subcontinent in the eighteenth century, were at the forefront when globalization first got going. Have we come full circle, with business taking over again from government?" Though picturing only one possible future, the scenario is scary.

Despite the growing economic clout of China and the heavy dependence of the U.S. economy on Beijing, Americans are still struggling to penetrate the Chinese mind-set—one that remains obscure and undependable despite close integration of the U.S. and Chinese economies through foreign trade and investments. The unsolicited $18.5 billion bid of the Chinese energy company CNOOC to take over a major U.S. oil company, Unocal Corporation, in 2005, further riled the White House, with many lawmakers calling for retaliation against a nation they believe has long flouted the rules of fair international trade. Representative Dana Rohrabacher (R) of California went so far as to call China a "Frankenstein monster" threatening U.S. interests.

In effect, China is increasingly emerging as a country that seeks to challenge the economic and military dominance of the United States in the United Nations and elsewhere. In its 2000 White Paper on Defense, China sharply criticized the prevailing power politics on the world stage, implicating the United States in no uncertain terms: "Certain big powers are pursuing neointerventionism, new gunboat policy, and neoeconomic colonialism, which are seriously damaging the sovereignty, independence, and development interests of many countries and threatening world peace and security in the process."

Some members of the American intelligentsia fear that China may soon emerge as a "kind of corporatist, militarized, nationalized state, one with similarity to the states of Mussolini or Francisco Franco." Professor David M. Lampton of Johns Hopkins has rightly described U.S.-China relations as being evocative of the Chinese adage "Tong chuang, yi meng," which translates to, "same bed, different dreams." No wonder, then, that on assuming office in 2000, one of the first actions of the Bush administration was to describe China as a "strategic competitor" and to label India as a "potential ally." Why would the United States want to keep all its economic eggs in a Chinese basket?

India's Tryst with the Dragon

For India, China is far from being a friendly neighbor and ally. Indian air force officer Air Commodore Jasjit Singh (Retired), a former director of the Institute for Defense Studies and Analysis, believes that "China, in collaboration with Pakistan, would always prefer India to be a low-impact nation." All moves to induct India as a permanent member of the UN Security Council have been perceived by China as a challenge to its own dominance in Asia. Even in 2005, when China finally said that it would support India's bid for a permanent seat, the Chinese scheme called for India to be deprived of the crucial veto power.

Dating from the fraternal stance of India-China under Nehru, termed "Bhai Bhai" (brothers), to the start of hostilities in the late 1950s when China publicly laid claim to areas along the northeastern parts of India, the relationship between India and China has fluctuated wildly. Today, India is still struggling with the trauma of the 1962 war, when China, in the guise of reclaiming territory, attacked India, catching her unawares and inflicting upon her a humiliating defeat. Decades after this Chinese "betrayal," the national humiliation still rings in our ears. China's subsequent 1964 nuclear test left India feeling all the more vulnerable and laid the foundation for India's own nuclear arms race.

In fact, Indian defense experts have a distinctive way of describing India's first nuclear test in 1974 during Indira Gandhi's regime. Called the Smiling Buddha test in deference to the fact that the Indian government claimed that it was a "peaceful" explosion, the experts acknowledge that the effort was mostly a retaliation and buildup against the Chinese nuclear program. China's strong alliance with archfoe Pakistan—which first resulted in the transfer of conventional weapons, and later, in the 1980s and '90s, in the reported transfer of nuclear and missile technologies from China to Pakistan—further hindered chances for a benign Indo-China relationship.

Indo-China relations reached an all-time low in 1998 when India conducted another nuclear test. The defense minister, George Fernandez—showing no fear for his politically incorrect tone—acknowledged that the tests were meant to act as a "long-term deterrent against China." As Indian analyst M. V. Rappai wrote in a paper for *Strategic Analyst*: "The Indo-China border dispute, China's support for Pakistan's WMD programs, the Chinese navy's increasing presence in the Indian Ocean, and the belief held by policy analysts that China will eventually emerge as a long-term competitor to India, all combine to further complicate Sino-India relations."

Besides, both American and Indian policymakers are also nervous about China's bid to militarize space with the testing of Beijing's first antisatellite weapon in January 2007. Add to that the joint Indo-U.S. concerns over maintaining peace and stability in Asia, oil and energy security, and economic overdominance of an authoritarian and possibly antagonistic China, and you get compelling reasons for a symbiotic relationship between India and the United States.

Small wonder, then, that the U.S. administration has implemented a seemingly well-thought-out strategy to engage India with this nuclear deal. India, too, on her part, has stretched out her hand toward the United States, despite many detractors of the deal within the Indian parliament. Clearly, the unspoken common bond bringing the two countries together is a nontransparent China's growing but unstated imperialistic ambition.

India and the United States—Growing Defense Cooperation

The nuclear deal may be a more contemporary issue, but with the Chinese threat looming large on the near horizon, combined with the growing menace of Islamic fundamentalism, Washington has been strategically engaging India militarily for some years now, with the goal of maintaining peace and stability in South Asia.

The military tango between Delhi and Washington began in earnest in 2001, when India strategically endorsed the National Missile Defense Program. Today, India and the United States are already working successfully as military partners in more than a dozen areas. The armies, navies, and air forces of the two nations have joined hands for operations in places ranging from the icy terrains of Alaska to the dark waters of the Arabian Sea, the guerrilla topography of Kashmir, the dense jungles of Mizoram, and the tropical heat of Agra.

The military cooperation on public display has seen the U.S. special forces and Indian paratroopers carry out the biggest-ever joint land and air exercises between the two countries, against the backdrop of the Taj Mahal, in May 2002; and the momentum has been on an upswing since, with the first joint combat exercise between the two nations in forty years taking place in February 2004.

Aimed at understanding each other's weapon and equipment capabilities and operating procedures, over the years these exercises have given India access to sophisticated defense equipment of the United States from India's active shopping list. While earlier India was allergic to presence of the American navy on the rim of Indian Ocean, today this presence is being actively solicited. India and the United States now share common concerns about the security of sea lanes through the Straits of Malacca and the South China Sea. "If you're looking at the security of the oil lanes or the sea lanes of Southeast Asia or the relationship with China, there is a natural convergence of interests from the United States and India on all this," says K. Santhanam, former director of the Institute for Defense Studies and Analysis.

From the perspective of the United States, America is at a juncture in history where it needs friends to fight terrorism and also allies to support its global dominance. Given India's love for democracy and liberal values, she could well emerge as the most trusted partner in both these areas.

But despite the intense defense cooperation, paranoia and misperceptions persist. A case in point is the 2002 report commissioned by the Pentagon. Compiled by Julie MacDonald, a director in the Joint Assessment Office of the Pentagon, this 141-page report is said to be a compilation of informal views of senior American defense officials. Titled *The Indo-U.S. Military Relationship: Expectations and Perceptions,* the report quotes a U.S. admiral as saying that both "the United States and India view China as a strategic threat . . . though we do not discuss this publicly," and adds that India could be that "friend" capable of assisting the U.S. military in dealing with the threat.

Despite that reservation, the MacDonald report points to America's strategic relationship with India as a hedge against losing significant allies such as Japan and South Korea. Americans interviewed for the report feared that Asia could become hostile and dangerous to a continuing American military presence in the region, and Washington's closer military ties with Delhi were intended to give the United States a "capable partner" (and one with a vast manpower base) to take on "more responsibility for low-end operations" in Asia.

George W. Bush is also looking at India as a potentially huge market for sale of its defense equipment. India is one of the biggest arms buyers in the Asia-Pacific region, and in a bid to upgrade its armed forces India's Defense Ministry is poised to spend more than $30 billion in importing weapons from foreign nations from 2007 to 2012. U.S.-based companies—especially Boeing, Lockheed Martin, and United Technologies—would indeed be looking forward to this opportunity, which comes close on the heels of India signing a defense agreement with Washington in 2005, followed by the civil nuclear deal of 2006. Aero India 2007 was one recent occasion when the world's best companies rushed to India. Held in the outskirts of Bangalore, the event saw companies like Boeing, Lockheed Martin, and Saab line up to showcase their finest wares to land orders worth billions from the Indian air force.

U.S. arms sales to India have jumped from $5.6 million in 2003 to $64 million in 2005. That's still a small percentage of the total, with Russia providing the bulk of India's arms purchases, supplemented by Israel. But all that is bound to change with Washington's new policy approach toward Delhi. Indeed, a Pentagon statement in March 2006 noted that "it is our goal to help meet India's needs in the defense realm, and to provide important capabilities and technologies that India seeks; we are on a path to accomplish this." That shift represents a revolutionary policy formulation for Indo-U.S. defense relations. From meager U.S. defense exports to India of only about $300 million in 2005, the numbers could now swell into double-digit billions.

Betting on India

If China is one of the glues that binds the Indo-U.S. defense and nuclear ambitions, the dragon is also an important reason for the growing economic cooperation between the two nations. The opportunities are diverse and the converging economic interests of the two nations make them appear even more lucrative.

Simply put, given China's growing ambitions, it makes sense for the United States not to become too close an ally of that communist country. To hedge its bets on the economic front, the United States needs access to the burgeoning Indian economy—perhaps the only emerging economy that can compete with China in the long run.

Already "China has been in the crosshairs of the Bush administration for pursuing policies that are said to hurt American companies and workers," according to a 2003 Knowledge@Wharton report. Some manufacturing companies are already leaning on the White House with complaints that the United States is under siege by China—the world's most populous nation, steaming with a red-hot economy, and currently a major supplier of goods to America. In fact, critics say that China dumps inexpensive goods in America that U.S. businesses simply cannot produce as cheaply, try as they may. There is also the contentious issue of China artificially keeping the yuan undervalued to undercut U.S. manufacturers, which is ruffling more than a few feathers in the U.S. Congress and Senate.

On the other hand, the growth potential of the Indian market is making American businesses even hungrier for a piece of the India pie. According to the India Brand Equity Foundation, "A majority of U.S. firms with an India presence are reporting double-digit growth today." That description fits GE, Bank of America, Motorola, Reebok, IBM, and many others. Some, like Coca-Cola and Citibank, have even declared the country to be their fastest-growing market globally. With many other American businesses waking up to the lure of the Indian market, it is little surprise that the establishment in D.C. is under pressure to keep relations with India on a strong footing.

The relationship between the United States and India is bound by a common commitment to freedom and tolerance. The two nations may still face tough times ahead in their budding friendship, but their shared commitments and values are bound to help them see their way through any difficult patches. Potent partners in matters military, nuclear, technological, and economic, Washington and Delhi look at each other and see a multifaceted future together; the two allies have so far only scratched the surface of their relationship.

CHAPTER 6

INDIA'S GROWING
GLOBAL MUSCLE

Time, they say, changes all things. That may be a cliché, but it's certainly a fitting description of what has happened on the international scene over the past couple of decades. Marxism is dead except in isolated pockets, and commercial interests rule foreign policy decisions. Globalization is continuing relentlessly across nations even as some voices of concern are being raised.

The Asian region has awakened from its prolonged slumber. China has already emerged as a superpower in the making, posing perhaps a strategic threat even to the United States. India is flexing her economic global presence as never before. Case in point: Feeling its muscle at the negotiating table for perhaps the first time since Independence, India sat down at the World Trade Organization meeting in July 2006, in Hong Kong, with new resolve. India's commerce minister said later that previously "India had been a mute spectator," but now they were demanding that the high farm subsidies of the United States and Europe be substantially reduced if they wanted India to offer further concessions. India was speaking up, and the major nations were listening and trying hard to get India to come around. The delegates from Delhi stood firm and that round of meetings failed. I believe this marks the beginning of a new era—a recognition that India is today a nation to be reckoned with.

I had an interesting conversation with Bill Emmott, who was editor of *The Economist* for thirteen years and is now an author in Delhi. During his visit in February 2007, he spoke at length about the painful geopolitics and geoeconomics that are driving globalization today. He said that the global paradox was most evident during the proceedings of the 2007 World Economic Forum at Davos. "One could sense a complete mismatch between the pessimistic forecast on the world political front and the great optimism about the economic forecast. Never before were the two so much in disconnect," Emmott said.

On the economic front, the last four years have seen a global GDP growth of between four and five and a half percent a year—the highest sustained average in the last forty years. The United States continues to "defy gravity," in Emmott's words, its economy remaining strong in spite of a high current-account deficit and negative savings rate. Germany and other euro countries are growing, and so is Japan after fifteen years of depression. Virtually all economically important nations are progressing well. Emmott argues that in the past, such huge economic growth could not have occurred alongside so much pessimism on the political front: terrorism spreading globally, war continuing in Iraq and Afghanistan with a possibility of spreading to Iran, oil prices triple of what they were five years ago. And to some extent globalization is threatened by protectionist moves, even on the part of Western countries, including the United States.

Emmott's answer: The old political scenarios don't work in today's world. Wars are isolated; terrorism, however bad at a human level, has no impact on economics; and strong growth in Asia has offset any major impact of oil and commodity prices. Indeed, that strong demand in Asia has helped spread the benefit of growth to resource-producing nations in west Asia, Africa, and Latin America.

Yet most major powers today are plagued by concerns over energy security, internal security, and military security, while geopolitical maneuvering continues between the developed and developing nations of the world.

So where does India fit into this picture of a shifting balance of power and changing strategic alliances? We'll tackle the question one slice at a time.

Challenges

Fundamentalist Islamic terrorism aside, the emerging twenty-first-century world order is unprecedented: never before have the affairs of nations depended so heavily on economic compulsions rather than simply the realpolitik of individual governments. The days of rigid enmities and alliances based on ideology have given way to a more worldly pragmatism of advancing national economic interests, dictating the economic and foreign policies of nations big and small. How else does one explain Washington's present-day tolerance of a Red China, despite the U.S. paranoia about containing Communism for all those years of the Cold War? Or the fact that Communist regimes like Vietnam are increasingly becoming market driven and beginning to look suspiciously like capitalist economies? Or that military dictatorships and authoritarian regimes like Pakistan, Thailand, and Myanmar sit freely across the table with democratic economies to discuss issues related to trade, market access, oil prices, and other global issues? In the long run, ideological frontiers are bound to become even more porous, giving way to a more market-driven, egalitarian world order than ever before.

Yet India will need to calibrate its relations with many other nations in the world to be able to further hone and tune her growing global stature. There are her immediate neighbors in the subcontinent—Pakistan, Burma, Nepal, Sri Lanka, and Bangladesh—some of whom are openly hostile about India's growing global clout. Meanwhile there's that growling tiger China, sharing a common border with India, smiling but with teeth bared.

India also needs to handle the complications of dealing with its old partner Russia, especially since India's sudden economic and military affinity with the United States and the emerging European Union seems to further threaten the once warm Russia/India ties.

Add energy security to this cauldron and the challenges facing India's foreign policy become even more daunting. India will remain an importer and huge consumer of energy, the needs growing inevitably with the country's increasing prosperity. Securing these growing levels of energy supplies will be an immense challenge.

All of these factors will dictate India's destiny, and because of them, the country's relations with other nations and blocs are changing in subtle and not-so-subtle ways. In each case the issues are different, demanding a tricky balancing act that can sometimes shift from month to month in the diplomacy required with each partner, ally, and adversary.

India and Israel: Transcending Traditional Mind-sets

Israel, as such a close and key strategic partner of the United States, is in ways a model of what India aims to become. For India, the reasoning is simple: If your brother and my brother are close friends, it makes sense that you and I become friends as well. It's almost inevitable and, from India's perspective, highly desirable, to build a solid foundation of trust and shared interests with Israel.

Since India and Israel established diplomatic relations in 1992, the two countries have inexorably moved close—a radical shift from India's earlier stance. Prior to that time, the country was an active supporter of the Palestinian cause and was one of the first non-Muslim and Arab nations to welcome Yasir Arafat—at a time when Israel, the United States, and many other Western nations considered him and his Palestine Liberation Organization to be a terrorist outfit. In the United Nations, India supported virtually every motion that asked Israel to vacate Palestine and other Arab territories it had captured during the wars in 1948, 1967, and 1973. Policy makers in Delhi viewed Arab states as "brothers" and supported all their causes in international forums, usually against Israel and the United States.

Since this shift, trade relations between India and Israel have skyrocketed. From $202 million in 1992, exports and imports between India and Israel touched $2.5 billion in 2005, with cooperation in technology-related R & D, agriculture, and nanotechnology boosting that total.

When India started inching closer to Israel after 1992, there was a huge debate in the Indian foreign policy establishment about the wisdom of the move. It was argued that moving closer to Israel would have two dangerous consequences. First, India would antagonize the oil-rich Arab states and jeopardize its future energy security, and also provoke Arab and other Muslim nations to openly support Pakistan in the ongoing Kashmir dispute. The second concern was the possible alienation of the huge Muslim population within India, which could hold dire consequences for the country's internal security.

But the proponents of a "get close to Israel" policy argued that no oil-rich state had ever denied oil to any country for having diplomatic relations with Israel. These advocates also pointed out that despite the numerous gestures of friendship and support to Arab and other Muslim nations, those supposed brother states had consistently supported Pakistan in the Kashmir dispute. Recriminations apart, the experience of the last decade and a half indicates that both worries appear to be ephemeral: oil supplies have not been disrupted, nor have the Arab states or India's local Muslim population been overly antagonized by India's relationship with Israel.

The shift in India's foreign focus came about not so much because Delhi turned its back on the Palestinian cause, but because of India's mounting cooperation with Israel in counterterrorism activities and sharing of intelligence. And then there's the business of military hardware: Israel became India's number two supplier of defense equipment, and still holds that position today. A 2003 report in the *Financial Times* conceded that the biggest reason why Delhi "quietly" strengthened relations with Israel was the threat of "growing Islamist terrorism in the divided state of Kashmir and elsewhere." The report went on to quote an Israeli official as saying, "There's a perception that both countries face similar threats and share similar experiences." Apart from Israel's providing India with the last word in war equipment like laser-guided bombs and unmanned aerial vehicles during the Kargil War to help flush out Pakistani infiltrators, it has also supplied India with sea-to-sea missiles and night-vision devices, among a host of other surveillance systems. Soon after Israeli prime minister Ariel Sharon's much-hyped visit to New Delhi, the year 2004 saw India sign a billion-dollar deal to acquire the sophisticated Phalcon early warning and control system from the Jewish nation.

As support for the proactive Israeli way of combating terror gains increasing acceptance in India, the momentum of this cooperation will continue to grow. And Israel will remain a key ally of India as the battle between terrorism and democracy intensifies in the years to come.

India and the Arab World: Oil Diplomacy?

In 2004, when the National Intelligence Council introduced their *Global Trends 2020* report at a press conference in Washington, D.C., readers of the report found the prediction that "China and India, which lack adequate domestic energy resources, will have to ensure continued access to outside suppliers; thus, the need for energy will be a major factor in shaping their foreign and defense policies, including expanding naval power."

Today, with those million new cars hitting the Indian roads every year, and new homes being built and sold at a record pace, energy needs have to be factored into every foreign-policy decision. Concerns about oil purchases and rising oil prices lock India into continued friendly relations with the Arab world. The United States, too, maintains a powerful presence in the Arab world for precisely the same reason.

Already the sixth largest energy consumer in the world, replacing France—and tipped to become the fourth largest by 2010—India can only see her energy concerns grow more and more pressing. With its booming economy, rapid industrialization, and rising population, India's energy consumption is pumping up at an average of eight percent a year. Currently, about thirty percent of those needs are filled from the country's own resources, but the experts are predicting that this figure may drop to less than ten percent by 2020. No wonder Indian energy firms are increasingly looking at foreign markets to develop new supply lines. Since a majority of India's oil import needs are presently met by the

Arab nations, any potential conflict in the already unstable region could bring the Indian economic growth to a grinding halt. This dependence is reason enough for India to seek alternative energy sources, which Delhi has been pursing through its growing diplomatic tête-à-tête with central Asian countries like Tajikistan, Kazakhstan, Azerbaijan, and Iran, in addition to current smaller energy suppliers including Russia, Vietnam, Myanmar, and African nations like Sudan and Nigeria.

Clearly, oil-rich regions, including Iran, will continue commanding great focus in India's foreign and economic policy for decades to come.

India and Iran: A Delicate Balance

Traditionally, India has shared excellent relations with Iran, another important source of future energy supplies. But that relationship now presents an acute dilemma for India's foreign policy establishment: There's no way that Indian policy makers can pretend to ignore the increasingly militant and fundamentalist stance taken by Iran against Israel and the United States, both budding partners on the international stage for India. The 2006 shootout between Israel and the Hezbollah in Lebanon clearly points toward a growing U.S. confrontation with Israel on the one hand and with Iran on the other. Add Iran's nuclear weapon ambitions and the cocktail becomes even more dangerous. There is a growing consensus within India's foreign policy establishment that an Iran with nuclear weapons will not be in India's strategic interests. Nuclear weapons are the reason India broke decades of traditional bonhomie with Iran and voted against the nation in February 2006, when the International Atomic Energy Agency (IAEA) censured Iran for its clandestine nuclear weapons program.

However, given the support for Iran among sections of the Indian political establishment, and Iran's huge untapped oil and gas reserves—said to be the second largest in the world—Delhi will be forced to tread a fine line between censure and cooperation with Iran in times to come. Add to that India's $22 billion liquefied-natural-gas deal with Iran; signed in 2005, in early 2007 the deal is still hanging in balance. Then there's the proposed Iran-Pakistan-India gas pipeline, which would be a big plus for the energy picture but also make Delhi's foreign policy dilemmas with Iran even more complicated. In fact, soon after the Indian PM voted against Iran at the IAEA resolution, he was forced to make a statement in the Indian Parliament stating that the vote did not "detract from India's traditionally close and friendly relations" with Iran. One can expect much more of such careful balancing from Delhi government offices in times to come.

India and Southeast Asia: Mutual Concerns

India's security interests lie not only in central and Southwest Asia, but also in the entire region stretching from the Gulf to Southeast Asia. India already boasts a strong cultural influence over Southeast Asia, in part a carryover from ancient times when large numbers of Indian warriors and traders migrated and settled in that region. During the British colonial rule, too, a large number of Indians were sent to the region to work in rubber, tea, and coffee plantations.

The cultural and social influence of India in Southeast Asia apart, Delhi's keen interest in the region stems from the huge trade and investment potential for its economy from partnering with the tiger economies there, particularly Thailand, Malaysia, Singapore, and Myanmar, with whom India even shares a land and maritime boundary. To further these ties, Delhi is rapidly forging ahead with its "look east" policy. Initiated in the early 1990s, this effort was regarded early on as an idealistic notion for stirring feelings of Asian brotherhood among the nations of the region. But it has turned into a concerted drive to build closer economic, political, and strategic ties with the Southeast Asian nations. Delhi is currently paving the way for a free-trade agreement that would boost bilateral trade with Thailand, Singapore, and Indonesia. Likely to be concluded soon, the agreement promises to drive growth for the entire region.

Another crucial binder for relations among India, Southeast Asia, and even Japan is the growing clout of China in that part of the world. As Singapore's minister mentor Lee Kuan Yew said in a December 2005 interview with *Time* magazine, "India would be a useful balance to China's heft." In fact, more than the United States or the European Union, it is Asian countries in close proximity with China that will be most directly affected as China gains economic might. To that extent, the nations of the region will need to hammer out a long-term strategy for engaging China in constructive ways.

India and Pakistan: Estranged Neighbors

Estranged brothers since 1947, India and Pakistan have been the worst of neighbors, on four different occasions descending into a shooting war. Pakistan is also the source of arms, training, and funds for repeated terrorist attacks on soft urban Indian targets. As noted earlier, in December 2001, Pakistani terrorists almost entered the

Indian Parliament on a suicide mission when the House was in session, killing twelve security personnel before they were gunned down. The incident very nearly started yet another war between the two countries.

Many Indians were hopeful that after 9/11, when Pakistan signed up as a full-fledged ally in the war on terror, there would be a slowdown in terrorist attacks on India from that direction. Those hopes have been dashed: Pakistan continues to support terrorist outfits whose principal cause is the "liberation" of Kashmir. Major world powers like the United States and United Kingdom are now coming to the conclusion that the Kashmiri terror outfits have close links with Al-Qaeda, and both countries have been putting pressure on Pakistan to quit all support to the terrorists. Complicating the situation, some analysts believe that certain rogue elements in the Pakistani armed forces, sympathetic to Al-Qaeda and its jihad against "infidels," are secretly continuing to provide support.

Hawks in the Indian foreign policy establishment have always demanded a tough line against Pakistan, including hot pursuit of terrorists into the Pakistan-occupied parts of Kashmir and cutting off all diplomatic ties with Pakistan. Thankfully, overall a more reasonable approach has prevailed: India and Pakistan continue to talk to each other, even though the dialogue often appears to be heading nowhere. Pakistan claims that relations between the two countries can improve only if the Kashmir dispute is settled. India insists that the Kashmir dispute can be discussed even as the two countries engage with each other on other fronts such as trade.

A model exists that India and Pakistan would do well to follow: the example set by Mexico and United States. Despite political differences, the two nations joined the North American Free Trade Agreement—NAFTA—which despite its many detractors has brought

A view of Ladakh, a region in the state of Jammu and Kashmir in northern India, renowned for its remote mountain beauty (*Hindustan Times*)

benefits to both nations. Similarly, India and Pakistan will have great economic potential to exploit if they bury their differences and join hands to promote bilateral trade, today tottering at a meager billion dollars—meager, at least, in terms of what it could be. Quantitative estimates made by various agencies put the untapped potential of two-way trade between the nations at nearly ten times the current level, giving a major boost to the textile, engineering, automobile, food grain, and entertainment sectors in both nations.

In the long run, it's in India's interests to have Pakistan as a neighbor that is not an implacable enemy, if still falling short of a friend. But for even that level of agreement to happen, the very system of governance has to change in Pakistan, which for most of its history has been ruled by a military that has a stake in keeping hostile feelings alive and nurturing hatred. Only when democracy becomes a reality in

Pakistan and the armed forces loosen their firm grip on all the levers of power can India really hope for enduring peace with Pakistan.

India and Russia: Friends Forever?

Historically, India and Russia have never really shared close ties—India's Soviet Tilt was never motivated by friendship or admiration, only by a pairing of needs. By the 1980s, the two countries were de facto strategic partners, and virtually the entire Indian military was dependent on arms supplied by the Kremlin. While the collapse of the Soviet Union and a rethinking of policies in Delhi has completely altered the equation, Russia continues to act as a friend to India—which is just as well, since India is still dependent on Soviet-era arms. Even today, more than seventy percent of India's weapons systems were purchased from Moscow, many of them still in use. And, as noted earlier, the connection still stands: the biggest defense suppliers for India today, accounting for over eighty-five percent of the total, are Israel and Russia.

For Moscow's part, a stronger India is in their strategic interests. Dmitri Trenin, deputy director of the Carnegie Moscow Center, hosted a seminar in 2003 on the prospects for India-Russia security relations. Speaking at the conference, Trenin acknowledged that the reason for Russia's interest in India is because of a "three-pronged security agenda": restraint on the proliferation of WMDs, the converging interests of India and Russia in Afghanistan, and India's role as a counterbalance to China in the region.

Thanks to the huge reserves of crude oil in Russia, Indian foreign-policy strategists are now also looking to Russia to ease their growing energy needs. Civil nuclear cooperation apart, India has a twenty-percent stake in the Sakhalin-I oil block in Russia, and Moscow is keen on Indian involvement in the Sakhalin-III project as well. More recently India's state-owned Oil and Natural Gas group signed a memorandum of understanding with Russian oil major Roseneft to jointly undertake oil-exploration projects, further signifying India's growing interest in Russia as a strategic source of energy in the long run rather than as a mere supplier of arms and weapons technology.

In January 2007, when Russian president Vladimir Putin visited his longtime friend Prime Minister Manmohan Singh, he said that energy security was the "most important of the emerging dimensions of our strategic partnership." A *Forbes* article called the visit a "road to renewing once tight ties," and true to that statement, as many as nine agreements were inked between the two nations during Putin's visit, in areas as diverse as energy, space, culture, and business, showing the present-day drive of the two nations to engage with each other.

India and the European Union: Budding Friendship

The European Union, busily expanding since its formation and now up to a formidable club of twenty-five nations across eastern and western Europe, is gradually emerging as an economically competitive force. Though the United States remains the front-runner in military might, there is little doubt that the European Union could emerge very soon as a strong contender for economic leadership. India can't afford to ignore the combined economic and strategic might of a dynamic EU.

Among the first countries in the world to establish contacts with what was then called the EEC, in the early 1960s, India limited her relations with the EU to trade and economic cooperation until 1994, when a cooperation agreement was inked. But it was the 2004 Hague

Summit that enhanced Indo-EU relations to a "strategic partnership" level and unleashed a new era in strategic and economic cooperation. Today, India routinely engages with the EU on disarmament, non-proliferation, UN reforms, and terrorism, enjoying a huge strategic edge in global politics.

There is palpable excitement in Indo-EU strategic circles about heightened cooperation in areas like trade, energy security, and space research. An Indo-EU energy panel is already in the offing; an agreement on India's participation in the EU's Galileo Satellite Navigation System—which hopes to compete with the American version, the Global Positioning System, as well as Russia's Global Navigation Satellite System—is being hashed out; and India's trade with member states of the EU is booming—the EU is India's largest trading partner, accounting for a quarter of her imports and exports.

Moreover, India's bilateral relations with individual nation-states in the European Union, especially with the United Kingdom, France, Germany, and Italy, are also on the rise.

Around Latin America

Brazilian forays with major Indian companies like Ranbaxy, TCS, Reliance Petrochemicals, and Tata Motors, among others, has led to a growing awareness in Delhi about the economic potential and strategic importance of Latin America. Indian policy makers have begun to appreciate the emerging profile of a great Brazilian market—the only Latin American country growing rapidly enough to be featured alongside India in Goldman Sachs's *BRICs Report*.

During his 2005 visit to Brazil, Manmohan Singh—the first Indian premier in four decades to visit there—called it a "voyage of discovery" and laid the groundwork for a potential win-win partnership with the Latin Americans. Also on the agenda was an initiative to boost the meager bilateral trade, currently shy of $3 billion.

Already partners in the G-4 efforts toward expansion of the permanent membership of the UN Security Council, India and Brazil have realized their strategic importance to one another. In particular, Delhi stands to gain from access to Latin America's oil and gas, biofuels like ethanol, and mining and forestry resources, making the region an alternative source of energy to feed India's burgeoning needs, which till now have been overly dependent on the Middle East. Even the recent surge of left-oriented leaders in Latin American countries poses no great risk to a geographically distant India. Clearly the mutual areas of strategic and economic cooperation may well be a "voyage of discovery" for the two nations.

Options

There are four powerful forces that are engaging the joint attention of the American administration and the Indian establishment and which they, as the two largest democracies, need to look at while engaging with the world in the next few decades. These forces are: the rising tide of global Islamic terrorism; the race for dwindling energy supplies; the impact of intensified globalization on weaker nations and calls for protectionism; and the growing threat of an unstable, nontransparent China.

So what are India's options in this emerging world order?

The first option, of course is to stay nonaligned, not becoming tied to any of the major power blocs emerging in the twenty-first century, which would be unwise—as is apparent from India's own decades of experience with nonalignment. Clearly, isolation does not pay any dividend. The second option is to forge an alliance with Russia and China and challenge the domination of America, reinforcing the romantic notions of many anti-imperialists, of Asian countries together ruling the world in the twenty-first century. But it is difficult to imagine India and China trusting each other to a point where they can become strategic allies anytime in the near future.

The third option is to become a close ally of the European Union. The EU does remain a powerhouse in the twenty-first century and can offer tremendous opportunities to India, both in terms of technology and markets. However, many analysts are skeptical about the future of the EU. Recent events in countries like France and the Netherlands have clearly shown that nationalistic tendencies are far stronger than the dream of a unified Europe and suggest that local politics will prevent EU countries from adopting policies that can take advantage of globalization.

The last option is the only viable one for India, the one India is already beginning to exercise: partnering with the United States. On key global issues, India shares converging interests with the United States Research in energy conservation and clean fuel—including clean coal energy plus alternative renewable sources of nonconventional energy like solar and wind—are areas where U.S. and Indian interests converge. Plus, their fates are already bound together insofar as containing terrorism is concerned. And, of course, the United States and India are already together in working to keep trade routes open globally while keeping at bay any demands for measures that would be overly protectionist.

As discussed elsewhere in this book, a strategic partnership between India and the United States will help in fighting terrorism, in tackling a possible problem of a China with expansionist goals, and in enabling capital and technology to flow freely to help solve global energy insecurity and provide handsome benefits of globalization to all.

India and China: Breathing Fire

After the United States, China will remain the second most important country for India. Though the historical wounds inflicted by the 1962 war have not been completely healed, both China and India seem to be moving on—they recently reopened the historic trade link that passes through Tibet. The Indian border town of Nathu La, in mid-2006 after nearly forty-four years, regained the role it had played for centuries as a busy, vital border post. In real terms, there is an explosive growth in trade between the two countries, with total value poised to exceed $20 billion in the next few years. China also seems to be willing now to recognize the state of Sikkim as part of India and is generally less hostile toward India in international forums.

However, India's foreign policy establishment is quite wary of the real intentions of China. For the last few decades, the Chinese seem to have been brilliantly successful in a strategy of containing India that would impede India's rise as a global power: military bases in Burma, open and continued support to Pakistan including providing it with nuclear technology, the courting of Bangladesh—all these tactics have been played by China to contain India.

Yet for the two nations to reap the benefits of globalization in the twenty-first century, this adversarial stance needs to be transformed. At the same time, the consensus within India demands that China be dealt with carefully. In fact, the deepening bond between India and the United States is a repeat of what happened in the 1970s when the

United States courted and befriended China (though primarily to contain the threat posed by the Soviet Union). I am convinced that China will inevitably threaten America's strategic interests in Asia and beyond; as suggested earlier, the growing ties between Delhi and Washington will strengthen India's role as a counterbalance to the growing threat of China.

By far the biggest thread stringing the futures of China and India together is the unparalleled economic rise of the two Asian powers in the twenty-first century. Trying to capture an accurate picture of how the two economies compare today, and the trajectory each is on, poses a set of fascinating challenges.

When Statistics Lie

It has become a favorite pastime of analysts and Asia watchers to compare India and China. Sure, some laugh at the notion of comparing these two up-and-comers, given the vast disparities in their respective GDPs, foreign investment levels, foreign exchange reserves, industrial production, and exports as a share of global trade. China is far ahead, while India totters way behind, despite both nations' starting on an equal footing merely a few decades ago: until 1980, the per capita incomes for the two countries were nearly on a par.

When you look only at the statistics, India does not appear in a particularly flattering light. Consider these figures:

- In 2005–2006, India's GDP of $796 billion was about one-third the official Chinese figure of $2.5 trillion. (On the other hand, to keep this picture in perspective, the GDP of the United States is $12 trillion plus—five times more than the Chinese figure.)

- China attracted more than $63 billion in foreign direct investments in 2006, while India managed only one-tenth of that figure.

- China accounts for about six percent of global trade, while India barely manages to touch one percent.

- Throughout the 1990s, GDP in China has grown at an annual average in excess of nine percent, while India's has grown at a comparatively meager average of six percent.

It's worth remembering that India is still clawing its way back from the stifling period of its Soviet-style bureaucratic stranglehold on the economy that ended in 1991. It took until 2001 for the Indian economic reforms to start bearing fruit; the Indian economy only slowly gained the trust of global investors and started drawing foreign investments to its transparent and efficient stock market, finally recording a blistering pace of annual growth at eight percent.

Flip through the figures on social indicators and India looks even more like a poor cousin: Literacy rates in India still hover around sixty percent, while China already boasts of a ninety-percent-plus literacy rate; the infant mortality rate for China is twenty-three deaths per thousand births, while India fares miserably at fifty-four deaths per thousand births; life expectancy in India is yet to cross sixty-five years, while for China it is nearly seventy-three years.

As far as figures tell, China is the clear winner.

But many analysts have begun to deduce that China's official statistics are, to put it politely, not entirely to be trusted. One leading voice of doubt is the respected professor Thomas Rawski of the University of Pittsburgh, author of *China by the Numbers: How*

Reform Affected Chinese Economic Statistics. He believes that ever since Beijing announced in 1998 the "great political responsibility" of achieving an eight-percent annual growth, China's statistical reporting has been buffeted by "winds of falsification and embellishment."

Tenzin Tsundue, a Free Tibet activist writing in *The Economic Times,* added that "there is no point in [India] competing with China, since [China] is boosting its economy by force. [India] cannot beat [the Chinese] in suppressing the millions and millions of poor workers and farmers at whose cost the economic balloon has been inflated. With no workers' rights [or] media freedom in PRC, the Beijing government can do anything they want. . . ."

In stark contrast, India's official figures are largely understated, thanks to that vast $50 billion parallel economy discussed earlier. If one were to take into account the total of mainstream and black income figures in India, the huge gap between the Indian and Chinese GDPs would lesson considerably.

The Global Competitiveness Report of Nations released by the World Economic Forum in September 2006 ranks India highest among all the BRIC countries at number forty-three, while China ranks a poor fifty-four in comparison. India ranks much higher than China on most "soft infrastructure" parameters, including enabling institutions for market economics, higher education, rule of law and political legislation, striving for efficiency, and building foundations of trust with foreign investors. Where India lost out in this report was in her grossly inadequate performance in health services for her teeming millions, as well as failures in primary education and infrastructure.

Here's a look at the Indian advantages over China, according to the report.

The India Advantage

- China has less chance for innovation in its relatively closed, state-controlled market. India has a democracy, a free market, and a free press, which empowers its people to be innovative and creative, even at the grassroots level.

- India's growing workforce of people below the age of twenty-five is a secret weapon in her arsenal, the benefits of which will soon start trickling in. China's one-child policy, on the other hand, while reducing the pressure of a population growing too fast, is making the nation age faster.

- Many Indians speak English; most Chinese don't.

- Both India and China are known for manufacturing, but India has lured many Fortune 500 companies to set up high-end Research & Development centers on her soil.

- India offers her citizens an open and free environment to replenish their minds and souls, in contrast to China's tightly regulated society.

Further Indian advantages lie in the country's proven scientific talent, research capability, enterprising attitude, niche managerial prowess, and great service-orientation.

Former *Economist* editor Emmott adds his own summation to this list. India's strength, he says, lies in its entrepreneurship, the global perspective of its leaders and managers, and its ability to manage complex global businesses. He points out, as well, that India has the powerful additional plus of "several generations of globally trained elite." Even the freedom fighters like Gandhi and Nehru, he notes, were British-educated.

Emmott also sees it as easy to draw the wrong conclusions from the BRICs report, which he insists are based on pure economic projections and, in the case of China, completely miss the political and societal instability. The study doesn't take into account how the rising wealthy population will react to their growing urge for political freedom and fundamental rights, nor how long the rural population will accept being largely left out of the new prosperity. While he doesn't see upheaval happening in China within the next ten or fifteen years, it's clear from Emmott's remarks that he believes political change to be likely, if not almost certain. The Soviet Union provides the model for a people rising up and throwing off the chains of a repressive society.

Now look at China's soft infrastructure indicators: Most of the so-called great buildings in China are government owned, and investments are barely going any longer into education, rural sectors, or the upgrading of industry. The cost of education is increasing and so is the dropout rate. What's more, productivity ratios and margins have been rapidly declining since the 1990s—precisely at the time when the shift from soft to hard technology became decisive. Yasheng Huang, author of *Selling China*, points out the rampant discontent among those in noncoastal China—villagers losing their land to authorities at abysmally low prices, an inefficient grievance redress system, quelling of dissent with an iron hand, and the miserable record on human rights.

Comparing the relative strength of India and China, the two rising powerhouses of Asia, is complicated by the tangled strengths and weaknesses of each. Yet overall, I believe that with its continued focus on soft infrastructure, India is set to soon surprise everyone with a growth model more sustainable than that of China, and that the positive payoffs to the American people accruing from their direct participation in the growth of the Indian economy may become the largest single factor for a major shift in focus of U.S. companies and their managers in the visible future.

Given India's stellar economic performance since 2001 and the chinks in China's armor, what does this say about the future balance of power in the region?

CHAPTER 7

UNDERSTANDING INDIANS

Philosophy, Attitudes, Etiquette

Not until we see the richness of the Hindu mind and its essential spirituality can we understand India.
   —Lin Yutang, Chinese writer and editor (1895–1976)

It may with truth be asserted that no description of Hinduism can be exhaustive which does not touch on almost every religious and philosophical idea that the world has ever known. . . . It is all-tolerant, all-compliant, all-comprehensive, all-absorbing. It has its spiritual and its material aspect, its esoteric and exoteric, its subjective and objective, its rational and irrational. . . . It has one side for the practical, another for the severely moral, another for the devotional and the imaginative, . . . another for the philosophical and speculative.
   —Dr. Sir M. Monier-Williams (1819–1899),
   Orientalist and scholar

When McDonald's decided to try breaking into the Indian marketplace, they thoroughly studied the moral and culinary food preferences before coming into the market with clever strategies. In this vast country, where tastes and diets differ greatly from region to region, the company devised not only the vegetarian menus described earlier, but also menus suitable to the various Indian customer preferences: no beef for Hindus, no pork for Muslims, but traditional Big

Macs in the parts of India where the majority of people eat beef. For vegetarians, the burgers aren't just meatless: they're prepared in "vegetarian only" kitchens with Indian flavors and eggless mayonnaise.

McDonald's had recognized the essential truth: The Indian identity thrives on difference and multiplicity, defying homogeneity at every level. Travel as little as fifty miles and everything changes: religious and spiritual beliefs, languages, dialects, dressing styles, mannerisms, customs, food—*everything*.

In other countries, even in parts of the United States, this kind of diversity can be a formula for suspicion, mistrust, prejudice, and the social ills that go along with those mind-sets. To some the diversity might be a warning that India is too complicated, confusing, or muddled—a place too layered even to think about trying to understand or do business with. In truth, though, this diversity has become one of the singular strengths of the country, a glue holding the nation together, and an essential piece of the puzzle for any foreign visitor to understand.

A Rainbow of Contradictions

Modern India takes pride in continuing its tradition of "unity in diversity." Every piece of paper currency, from the ten-rupee note to the thousand-rupee bill, has language printed on it in all (over a dozen) official scripts. Henry Higgins, Shaw's fictional linguist from *Pygmalion* and *My Fair Lady,* sharpened his skills in India, where the folks in neighboring towns speak different dialects, and an official tally puts the number of major dialects at more than fifteen hundred.

Even minor restaurants serve up a range of cuisines from at least four regions of the country; women drape sumptuous six- to nine-yard saris in no fewer than a dozen different ways; the variety of indigenous textiles, art, and crafts seems endless; and Hindus, Muslims, Buddhists, Jains, Sikhs, Parsees, Christians, and Jews can be seen offering prayers in their own unique, traditional manner.

India thrives on contradictions like no place else; any visitor, tourist, or business representative can expect the unexpected. Relying on a trusted Indian friend to act as buffer and to protect one from culture shock is helpful in this sometimes highly confusing country. At your hotel, they may not serve beef because of the reverence Hindus hold for the cow. Yet you may hear the conversation of a Hindu man from Kerala seated at a nearby table telling his wife on a cell phone that he will return home tomorrow and would prefer a beefsteak for dinner. In the morning you might run into a purist who would not marry anyone related to him through any of the ten previous generations—a common requirement in north India. In the evening, you might meet another purist from the south of India who would only marry his daughter to one of her uncles.

In a temple, where you might expect more familiar rules and behavior, you could be truly shocked to witness a sadhu (a holy man who customarily wears orange) amble in nonchalantly, completely nude. However, your Indian guide will hardly see any cause for panic. Rather than calling the police, he may instead prostrate himself at the sadhu's feet.

Chances are your host will not even stop to justify or explain what you have seen; even if he's well educated, he will likely have consulted his horoscope before stepping out to face the day, and will later join the queue for the blessings of a holy man. And if you have an accident or fall ill, don't be surprised when the urbane doctor tells you to pray for health instead of giving you medicine.

Historically, Indian identity arises out of a complex skein of many strands—Islamic invasions, British subjugation, Christian conversions,

Sadhus on a ghat (steps) in Varanasi, a famous Hindu holy city situated
on the banks of the Ganges River   (*Stephen Haynes*)

Hindu tolerance, Sikh orientation to service, Sufi inspiration, Buddhist
dedication without ritual, and many more woven into a friendly and intelligent tapestry of culture. Somehow India itself, like the henna fo-
liage that grows here in profusion, always comes out with better colors
after each grinding—with the result of an unmatched blend of beauty,
courage, resilience, tolerance, optimism, and an ever-readiness to adapt
and change.

"Every time I come to India," says J. C. Carrière, the Indophile
French writer, "I know before the plane lands that I am going to see
something that I have never seen before—maybe a minor detail,
sometimes the behavior of someone. A new place, a new concept.
Which is not the case when I go to New York, for instance. I am not
expecting to be surprised. I know the country and that everything
follows certain rules. Here, it changes, all the time."

This is even true for me, though you would think nothing could surprise me in my own home country. But just the other day, I was visiting a palace-turned-hotel with a guest, and we saw three people atop a tree. They were bent over to examine the leaves. When asked what they were up to, they dutifully replied that they were "tree leaf cleaners." In India, we care about our trees—but I had no idea the concern went that far.

Still, that unexpected occupation fits the pattern. Everything in India seems to come in an almost limitless variety. Detailed treatises on love, duty, drama, music, economics, or even the art of stealing, list every possible aspect of their subjects. From creating millions of yogic postures to categorizing melodic scales to suit every hour, every season, every mood, the Indian mind is forever searching. In literature this search takes the form of the classic plot-within-a-plot strategy of the Indian epic; in the classical performance arts, the endless ways in which even fingers and eyeballs are made to dance.

Years of colonial rule have left lasting imprints on Indian society. The waiter at a five-star hotel will serve the foreigner first and bestow a wider smile. The CEO's secretary will give you the earliest appointment while a poorer Indian cousin might have been waiting for weeks. Speaking fluent English gives instant status as "educated" and "elite." Even sixty years after independence, "Queen's English" rules in administrative correspondence.

Centuries of foreign rule have made Indians passive recipients of orders and edicts. For Americans, the passive patience of Indians can be quite baffling; some consider it a form of mystical Oriental fatalism. You will find Indians waiting patiently for hours to be attended to at a government office, a hospital, a bank, even a post office. Fortunately, the younger generation is faring much better—working with greater confidence, overcoming the shackles of the British era to regain pride and poise once again.

Indophile Dominique Lapierre remains convinced that it is "the Indian's capacity to adjust and overcome [that] is driving its society forward." When Mumbai was completely flooded like New Orleans, it took the city less than twenty-four hours to get the power on, albeit through short-circuiting many safety nets and practices.

From beggars to billionaires, from saints to charlatans, from rickshaws to Jaguars, from cows to cafés, from shanties to palaces, from perfection-seeking yogis to mediocre consumerist yuppies, the profusion of contrasts in India is mind-boggling indeed. For companies interested in this market of a billion people, or any individual interested in grasping the complexities of this fascinating mix of cultures, here's a short primer on the nature of the Indian character.

The Multitasking Indian

As an undergraduate, I used to see the waiters at our Delhi University café—usually overcrowded with rushed, demanding students—relying on another amazing and amusing talent common among Indian workers, a talent I suspect grows out of cleverly overcoming the disadvantage of the millions who need to work but who cannot read or write. These waiters would take individual orders from ten or a dozen customers at one table, writing nothing down, then stop at other packed tables and take their orders as well, yet deliver every dish correctly. Unable to use pad and pencil, they have over generations developed memories that would put the rest of us to shame.

(I think I have spotted one aspect of that memory talent that has become part of every Indian's heritage. In the United States, phone numbers are written and spoken in small groups of digits that are easily remembered: 212-555-1927. In India, the phone numbers have eleven or twelve digits, but you see them on advertising posters all over the country written in a solid block: 1124184719, for example. I think Indians have developed the ability to see a number like that and almost instantly commit the entire string to memory, a talent we have somehow acquired from our illiterate brethren.)

Another unexpected talent shared by many Indians frequently gives me a laugh: I love to watch the amazement of foreigners when they come across a worker such as a passenger agent at an Indian Airlines check-in counter. They see one lady dividing her attention among a flock of anxious, animated customers who crowd around her as she simultaneously juggles ticketing for one person at her computer while handing another's over-baggage issue and responding accurately and helpfully to the queries of several of the others squeezing into the space in front of her counter. Standing patiently in line for your turn at the counter is virtually unheard of in India, because it's unnecessary.

These inherent abilities for multitasking, multiprocessing, and diverse thinking—reflections of our diverse multicultural environment—are strengths that contribute to making India a talent hub. The spiritual and cultural heritage of the Indian people empowers them with an innate sense of action to deal with all kinds of challenges and situations—an ability greatly valued in the business world.

This multitasking talent often evokes amusing reactions from others. I've sat in business negotiation meetings in Japan unaccompanied by any associates, where I would deal with one of the Japanese team on finance, another on manufacturing, others on marketing, technology, and machinery. For an Indian, this multitasking is an everyday ability. The Japanese, looking dumbfounded, would always ask why I had not brought a team with me.

These abilities have become genetically ingrained in all of us.

The Caste System

The much-rallied-against caste system is not a part of Hinduism—even Muslims and Christians in India have it. Started as an Indian social system of harmoniously aligning different talents in society, the original plan was not to create hierarchy but to make room for all kinds of individual competencies: Brahmins (priests) doing their duty to guide the spiritual evolution of society through their example of following the righteous path; the warriors and kings doing their duty as protectors; the merchants and traders providing goods to all; and the laboring class providing services and support for society's functioning. This system provided equity for all and was not exploitive at any level. Over time, this well-functioning system was corrupted by a grab for power and privilege, especially by the priests and kings, leading over the years to the caste system of today—made even worse when politicians stir resentments with "caste-based politics." Though the caste system was clearly to have been rendered illegal by the Indian constitution in 1950, it still survives.

The caste system flourished for centuries, defining the religious and social fabric of Indian society. Later another category evolved: the "untouchables"—mainly relegated to work that involved cleaning up filth and excrement, leading to the attitude that for an upper-class individual to get anywhere near people of these castes would be contaminating or polluting.

In 1935, the British government prepared a list of all socially deprived classes, with the aim of increasing their representation in legislature and government jobs, referring to them in classic governmentese as "Scheduled Castes." This label is still used in all government records.

In the 1990s, many self-aware individuals from these castes began referring to themselves as Dalits (the oppressed), and the name has largely stuck in popular use. Another label for people at the bottom of the social hierarchy is "OBCs"—which, believe it or not, stands for "Other Backward Classes," a leftover from the British Raj. The term actually refers to any group discriminated against in their own region of the country; in regions where they are in the minority, even Brahmins can be OBCs.

Over the centuries, massive oppressions of the Scheduled Castes have forced many lower-caste Hindus to resort to converting to another religion—Christianity, Buddhism, or Islam—in hopes of escaping the prejudices and oppression of the "untouchable" tag. A recent trend shows thousands of lower-caste Dalits routinely attending mass ceremonies to convert. In one such ceremony in October 2006, Joseph D'Souza, president of the Dalit Freedom Network, told the BBC that "I think it's important to understand that this is a cry for human dignity, it's a cry for human worth." In fact, D'Souza himself is a Christian convert. But even in such cases, experiences that have been made public have shown that after conversion, the Dalits' lot has not bettered substantially.

While prejudices certainly remain, as they do against blacks in America, Dalits are by law given preference, with twenty to thirty percent of jobs reserved for them in government and educational institutions, and affirmative action in their favor being insisted upon even in the private sector.

Today even at the lowest levels of society, people understand the law and are fighting back. In October 2006, in Chandan Nagar village in the northern border state of Bihar, Dalit women launched a protest to reinstate their right to worship. Their anger was targeted at the local priest of the temple, who refused Dalits entry into the temple premises and threw away their offerings to God. In this case, thanks to the support of the local administration, these Dalit women were successful in removing the priest from his office, and a Dalit was appointed as the head of the temple committee.

The example in Nagar demonstrates that the situation is improving with a political and social awakening, as the Dalits and OBCs are becoming aware of their human rights. Yet eradication of the tiered society of India is not going to happen rapidly; nearly sixty years after the caste system was legally abolished, it continues to define the lives of millions of Indians who are, incredibly, divided into more than a few thousand castes and subcastes.

The caste system leaves India saddled with one of its many contradictions: a society surging ahead to take its place as one of the world's great economic powers, while stuck with a social system that is like something out of the dark ages.

The Dedication to Service

India's growing stature globally as a service economy is no fluke. The ethos of service is firmly ingrained in the Indian way of life, inasmuch as service to others is considered a means to attain one's own salvation. It is not uncommon to see the well-to-do distributing cooked food, fruit, clothes, or money on festival days and even on special days of the week. The temples of the Sikhs—the community most known for its commitment to service—feed millions of poor Indians every day free of cost. The huge communal kitchens are kept up by generous donations from people in the local area.

India is also the land of saints and mystics—gurus—who lead thousands of different spiritual organizations. The man I consider my own guide and guru, Sai Baba, runs a charitable organization funded by private donations. The organization has built colleges offering value-based education, and hospitals providing one-hundred-percent free services to poor people. It has even brought drinking water to the parched lands of the Anantpur District. Spiritual masters occupy a central place in every Indian household and community. This informal spiritual sector provides not just food but hope as well to the millions of poor, in a country that has never provided a state-run social security net.

Whatever the motivation, service to society is seen as a means to serve the self by bettering one's own Karma and expanding one's own heart and consciousness.

In fact, such is the pull of the ethic of service and charity that it is not surprising to find even beggars in India bidding to improve their next incarnation by giving away a sizable fraction of their "incomes." Temples here receive a greater percentage of funds from donations made by the people in remote rural villages than from those in the cities.

Why the Have-Nots of India Don't Envy the Haves

Diversity in India has not given rise to the kind of multiculturalism espoused by the West. Whereas in the United States, policies upholding multiculturalism aim at the ideal of equality for all, in India the contention is not so much of equality among different cultural strands but rather acceptance of the other and the recognition of different social realities.

When in India, you never need to be "politically correct"; you can voice your opinion freely. It is through this understanding of another person's reality that the haves and the have-nots deal with one another, in an unsentimental sort of a way: the empathetic CEO might draw ambitious plans for affirmative action for the poor in his neighborhood but may not offer a penny to the roadside leper. Likewise the street kids may implore you one minute with pity-soliciting looks and in the next minute pluck out a flower from their on-sale wares, offering it free in admiration for a pretty girl.

The Vedanta

The Indian mind-set mirrors the complexity of India herself. An Indian can hardly be reduced to a single linguistic or national identity. Indians and Americans share a unifying spiritual heritage that espouses respect for diversity and peaceful coexistence through means of mutual respect, accommodation, flexibility, and adaptability.

The Indian has remarkable composure when confronted with extremely different ways of praying and living; all contradictions are held together in the protective lap of pan-religious tradition. The school of thought that Indians call "Vedanta" provides the strong glue that cements all levels and corners of the diverse Indian society into one, even as the modernizing currents of material growth take hold. Understanding the essence of what is meant by Vedanta is fundamental to understanding the Indian mind.

The Vedanta is the world's most ancient philosophy (though in some ways it can seem downright postmodern). It is utterly accepting of pluralism and multiplicity, minus any dogma whatsoever. Vedanta carries the essential teachings of the Vedas, the basis of Sanatan Dharma, now called Hinduism.

The underlying beliefs of Vedanta are that every human is a reflection of Godhood, the supreme energy. Therefore, all religions, beliefs, and perspectives of Truth are equally valid. The Vedanta says that we humans—unlike animals that are on lower rung of consciousness—have the possibility, in this life and in next reincarnations, of either realizing our innate divinity or falling from the ladder of consciousness, through our own Karma.

The energy of beings, Vedanta says, cannot be restricted to limited individual egos. Humans carry in them the infinite energy of the universe. Just as a drop of water shares the same reality as that of the ocean with which it merges, so, too, the human soul has only to realize its inherent divinity, by removing the veil of illusory existence—the day-to-day level of consciousness—through any of the various paths of yoga (which means "union" with the Ultimate).

In the United States, yoga is largely accepted as a physical activity—with focus primarily on its challenging postures and weight-reducing effects. But in India, yoga contains the entire menu of realization—its practice here must traverse the physical, emotional, and mental "sheaths" to ultimately bring out the realization of the hidden divine core within each of us. Seeking this core, this center point of balance—for our body, emotions, actions, and reflection—is the very aim of sustained yogic practice.

This yogic realization is attained when the individual soul is plugged into the infinite source of energy and a connection is established. Only then are we liberated from dualistic perceptions of misery/happiness, mine/thine, life/death.

Indians view death as a continuation of life: despite the demise of the physical body, the subtle life force, the soul, lives on. Just as we shed childhood to enter youth, and youth to enter old age, in this same way we shed old age to enter death, and step into rebirth once again, until ultimately the soul is "realized" and attains liberation by merging with the infinite Source of all creation.

In Vedanta, your "realization" is the only Truth to seek: no other-worldly God to impress, no other Truth to attain beyond yourself. Vedanta, then, is not a religion at all. It is an all-embracing and emancipating view and way of life. The multiplicity of gods and deities often makes the foreigner think of the nontheistic Hinduism as being polytheistic. Yet these images are nothing but man's way of getting the idea of divinity down to his level.

Swami Vivekananda (1863–1902), one of the most famous spiritual leaders of the philosophies of Vedanta, said, "If a person wants to drink milk, he uses a cup, as he cannot drink it directly from the source. Idols are nothing but symbols through which divinity can be comprehended. An idol helps undeveloped minds to grasp high spiritual truths." Indians will sanctify anything—cattle or stone—if it helps them understand a higher truth.

Anyone can be Vedantic, whether he worships a deity or not. He needs to realize his own higher nature—by walking any of the existing yogic paths, or even by inventing another one that suits his sensibility better. The diversity of religious faiths and yogic paths of India reflects this continuous search of Indians for truth through whatever route seems to work for the individual.

Unlike the Christian concept of man as sinner, Hindus consider man divine. In contrast to the Islamic faith, nothing is pagan or blasphemous in the Indian sphere; the most daring of spiritual traditions are tried, tested, and perfected here.

If you travel from West Bengal to Tamil Nadu, it is like going to a totally different country. The people don't dress the same, eat the same, or speak the same language. But they all know the Mahabharata. *Whereas if you go from France to Germany, there's nothing in common, not even an epic. In that sense, epics like the* Mahabharata *are the invisible cement that binds India into one. For us, it was a great surprise to see how cohesive this cement actually is. Even Muslims in India know the* Mahabharata *and refer to it.*

—J. C. Carrière, French writer/director

Dharma and Karma—the Twin Pillars

In India you don't need to mind your Ps and Qs. Just mind your Ds and Ks: Dharma and Karma, the twin pillars of Vedanta.

Dharma

"Dharma" broadly means your spiritual duty to the Self in accordance with your nature, station, and situation in life. To follow your human Dharma means to be guided by your higher nature, given your circumstances. An older person's Dharma may be different from that of a younger man, a rich man's different from that of a beggar.

Dharma can broadly be described as one's Purpose and Duty in Life—the search for one's unity with God through the practice of "right conduct" in day-to-day life, upholding the "larger good." But right conduct, in the Vedantic sense, does not carry the dualistic sense of right conduct in contrast to wrong conduct. Rather, right conduct is characterized by listening to the inner voice of your conscience.

Dharma, for the Indian, means doing the "right" thing as one sees it—not necessarily in an absolute moral or ethical sense as is so often the case in the West. Importantly, one person's right action, arising from his Dharmic impulsion, may be different from another's, or even at cross-purposes with it, but that is precisely the point: in playing out our respective Dharma, dictated by our innate and inherited sense of duty and call of conscience, we all end up acting as the appropriate conduits for the Creative Force, God, to flow through us; in this way, we play out, with our respective roles, the larger plan of Life. If an Indian were to choose between right actions as espoused by law and as dictated by his conscience, chances are he will choose the latter.

This stance of allowing each person to act in accordance with his respective conscience is key, then, to the Indian acceptance of multiple realities. Nothing shocks, because there is no single ideal of Reality and Truth to uphold. In fact, for the Indian, Reality by definition implies the acceptance of Multiplicity and Relativism, of a diverse set of people, their circumstances, their conditions, their responses.

Karma

"Karma" refers to your actions in this life and, for an Indian, actions in your previous lives. To follow one's Karma means to engage in action for the sake of the action itself, without expectation of the result. It means a hundred percent involvement, with zero percent attachment.

This balance means accepting that one cannot control results because results emerge only as the sum total of a lot of other influences—our Karma, someone else's Karma, the land's Karma, the earth's Karma, our previous generation's Karma. Take 9/11 or Katrina in New Orleans, for example: devastation wreaked havoc and suffering among innocent people through no fault of theirs. In India, we'd say they were meant to bear a Karmic debt. The universe, Indians consider, never retains anything or takes any energy, good or bad. It only gives back what we humans have given it from time to time in terms of positive or negative energy.

As mentioned, the terms *Dharma* and *Karma* are understood and practiced by all—educated and the illiterate, of every faith. The Christian maidservant will wail about her earlier bad Karma if her alcoholic husband beats her every night; a Sikh woman will stoically endure the death of her young child in a road accident, taking her suffering to be a result of her previous bad Karma; and the rich Jain trader will thank his accumulated bank balance of good Karma over previous lives for present fortunes, and he'll do good deeds—building hospitals or temples, offering free food—to keep intact his "bank balance" of good Karma.

If Karma makes Indians accept all kinds of things, it also drives them to engage in action on their own, uncomplaining about lack of this or that. A European friend visiting Varanasi, the spiritual sanctuary of India, remarked to me that in India even the poorest of people are always busy doing something, not waiting for a miracle to just happen.

So if the Vedanta, Dharma, and Karma are fundamental in the landscape of every Indian, how do they actually translate into attitudes of daily life?

Key Indian Attitudes

Individualism: the Space for Community

Belgian-born artist and writer Henri Michaux (1899–1984) observed with great insight in his Oriental-travel memoir, *A Barbarian in Asia,* that a "good" Hindu hardly worries about any other than his own salvation. The Indian ethos of the individual soul's liberation from the endless cycle of birth and death does indeed create an extreme preoccupation with the development of the self, in a rather independent and at times extreme sort of way. Buddha left his wife for the jungles without whispering a word (the beautiful poem "Yashod-hara," by Maithili Sharan Gupta, captures the pain of the deserted wife's plight).

Yet the Indian brand of individualism lacks the rigid frontier between "me" and "him." In the United States, for instance, a person alone at home would say, "I'm alone"; in India, "No one is home" would probably mean your uncles, aunts, cousins, and grandparents are out for lunch, leaving you *and* your parents *and* your siblings unaccompanied and therefore "alone" (!). Similarly, while an American woman would meet her doctor even without her husband, her Indian counterpart would be accompanied by husband, brother, mother, and daughter, at the very least. Whatever would be considered "other" in the West—anyone other than oneself—are all assimilated in the Indian's "relational individualism."

The Westerner considers the individual himself as the seat of identity; Indian individualism thrives on links with the family and the community. In the United States, where one would just call 911 upon witnessing a road accident, a similar event on Indian roads, no matter in which part of the country, will draw people to the site of the accident in no time. And by the time the police arrive, the patient will have been driven to the hospital by some Samaritans, who would have paid the admission fee, called up the relatives using the victim's cell phone, and driven off to work. (See any Bollywood flick and you will notice that the police always arrive after the situation is well under control.)

And Indians don't just reach out in moments of crisis. If you're passing a village in your Jeep and are looking for some water, in just a matter of minutes you will be offered what you need by a villager; though he may earn only twenty dollars a day he will miss work in order to provide you with a meal, even if it means using food his family needs, and will refuse any payment.

Joint Families: Daily Dose of Excitement

An average Indian household will have at least three generations living in it. In rural areas, separate bedrooms for couples are uncommon. But the couples don't seem to mind. They deal with this issue just as they might deal with any other. Of course, in some cases living together is the decision of a traditional family with close ties; in other cases it has more to do with the family members not being able to afford separate housing. (Or sometimes they're waiting for a property title dispute to be settled by the courts—which could take a lifetime.)

The Indian, conscious of tradition, is at all times ready to build a relationship with family, community, and society. Even if the relationships are a far cry from being perfect (mostly the case in today's tormented times), the Indian will hardly feel torn over it: in the morning, he will bow to touch the feet of a senior business mentor who is "brother" to him, yet be seen battling out a vicious court case with the same man in the afternoon; he will enjoy a convivial dinner with his siblings, parents, nephews, and nieces, even exchange gifts at festivals, and yet prattle on among his friends about all his dislikes of and frictions with his family members.

Privacy in India

A foreign author observes: "There is very little privacy in an Indian household, nor does it seem to be missed or much desired. Indians as a rule appear to have less-developed privacy needs than do Americans, and usually miss the bustling human contact. . . ."

If staying with an Indian host, know that at the end of the very warm visit—you have been fed to no end, asked details about your personal life, advised on the color of your tie—you, too, will have been assimilated into the family as a son, brother, or sister. Consider this a compliment; this means they like you and will keep their doors always open for you—just as they would for their family members. And no need to thank your foster family; they're doing you no favors—they consider this as their least duty, their Dharma.

That brings us to the itchy issue of privacy about personal matters. If you're coming to India to attend a friend's wedding, expect to be asked, "Are you married?" by graying grandmas, elegant ladies, little menaces, cousins of the bride and groom. I pose the same question to women candidates at job interviews, since a married woman is much more likely to quit because of family responsibilities, and no one stands on the right to privacy.

Unlike Westerners, Indians have not inherited the idea of privacy as essential. This difference may explain why even elite Indians in swanky sedans roll down their windows to smilingly ask passersby for directions, even if they have a detailed city map in their hand. They need the reassurance of the "bustling human contact."

Many a foreigner has lamented the "typically Indian" disrespect for waiting in line and the obsessive predilection for descending like a nuclear cloud on any single window counter. An American friend visiting the Ranthambore Wildlife Sanctuary was at a loss for words when he discovered that the Indian drivers, instead of simply forming a line and smoothly driving in one at a time, would completely jam the entry gate with their taxis, advancing into the slightest space available between the bumper of the car in front and the headlights of the one behind.

But this problem was not just about the lack of queue temperament. What completely stumped our friend was the fact that this problem of hysterical clogging was not an exception: it occurred every single day, with the agency with the same set of seventeen drivers who had escorted tourists daily for God knows how many years. These drivers know each other like family: they play cards as they sit huddled under the shade of a tree, ogling in unison at the same short-skirted foreign woman, and yet drive out the next morning in their taxis and screech and bellow at one another at the entry gate. Indians seem, then, to be at home with mayhem. The crowd is their energy source.

In public, the Indian is ever ready to forge an instant relationship without seeking the promise of its continuity—offering eye contact to the person next to them at the railway ticket counter, addressing a stranger as "sister" or "brother"—rickshaw puller, milkman, vegetable vendor, grocer, waiter, peon, and watchman are "brothers" to all. (This custom is particularly useful for a foreigner who has just been over-charged or cheated by a man who seemed to be trustworthy because his English was good enough to give him the air of being upper-class and prosperous: For help, call out to any illiterate, addressing him as "brother"—or even better, using the Hindi word, "bhaiya"—and you'll get back much more than you expected, resolving the problem with the man who cheated you, and perhaps even being provided lunch and practical tips for the culturally challenged.)

Indian Communication

In many households it is not unusual to find under one roof a Punjabi father, a mother from Uttar Pradesh, a cook from Bihar, a maid from Kerala, and a daughter studying at a Christian convent school.

Indians live and deal with diversity of languages, accents, rituals, and more from their first day on in the world. A Frenchman only needs to be able to speak, read, write, and understand French; in England, only English. In India, however, there is nothing like a unifying "Indian language," only a profusion of languages. Even couples from across cultures (a Malayalee married to a Punjabi, say) do not converse in their respective mother tongues, and their offspring often inherit English as their mother tongue. Adaptability and flexibility are built into the psyche from the very start. That's the latitude of the Indian mind.

Even a local postman (who may have finished only the equivalent of middle school) can decipher the most cryptic of clues hidden in among the mysterious accents, phonetics, and spellings of the letters he is in charge of delivering; one local letter carrier had an envelope in his stack addressed to "Science Tipon College, New Delhi." But there is no such place. With little waste of time, he deduced that it was actually meant for a New Delhi college called St. Stephen's. The flexible, problem-solving Indian mind at work.

Are Indians Rude?

Modern Mumbai was recently ranked the rudest city in the world, punching right in the solar plexus all claims to Indian "service orientation." Upset Indians strongly challenged the survey's findings and upheld the people of Mumbai ("Mumbaikars") as friendly, polite, approachable, and helpful.

German Indologist Max Müller understood even back in the late 1800s what it is that Westerners see as rudeness. His research led him to conclude that what Hindus show is not rudeness but strength. The ancient Hindu's emphasis on courteous speech springs from the Hindu's view that rudeness of speech is a sign of bad breeding and lack of knowledge. Even today, Indians from all backgrounds value hospitality, generosity, service, altruism, and courtesy.

Television commercial producer Prahlad Kakkar, interviewed in an article for the BBC, explains this difference in opinion as due to the Western criteria used to assess politeness in India (or anywhere in Asia, for that matter). Included in the judging was whether people opened doors for others in public buildings, whether they helped pick up papers dropped on a busy street, and whether a shopkeeper said thank you when a purchase—big or small—was made. Kakkar rightly concludes that the reason for the poor score of Asian cities on the politeness scale is due to cultural differences. For instance, regarding the criterian of saying thank you after a purchase, Indians (and other Asians too) consider it an important part of a transaction, but their expression of it may be nonverbal, like smiling, nodding the head, bowing slightly, or making the gesture of Namaskar (hands folded in the prayer position).

Another author points out, "When an Indian tells you, 'Give your passport,' or, 'Stand there in that line,' without the usual courtesy of 'please,' he or she isn't being rude. Most Indian languages have no specific word for *please;* it is expressed in the verb itself when using the polite form of address, and the tone of the instruction often conveys an implied 'please' that might easily be missed by a Westerner but would be clear to any Indian."

Australian Simon Hildebrand, who has been the country manager in India for an Australian warehousing and transportation company and is currently being posted to Korea, would also disagree with the survey's findings; he says, "When I go [to Korea], I would like to take some bits of [India] with me. I would like to take the openness, [the] willingness to learn and listen, with me. This is not something found in other cultures around the world. And that is what makes India, more specifically Mumbai, a pleasant place to live in."

Doing Business in India: Tuning in to the Etiquette

Professor Mary Munter, of the Tuck School, Dartmouth College, and author of the popular *Guide to Managerial Communication,* while delivering a guest lecture at our Media College in New Delhi, talked about the respective strengths of Indians and Americans. Indians, Munter said, are more skilled than Americans: they speak more languages; they tend to be more open-minded and accepting; and they carry the spiritual dimension. Americans, on the other hand, have mastered the balance between the extremes of aggressiveness and submissiveness, and are more organized and pragmatic. Another view comes from Ranjan ji Sinha, an Indian entrepreneur and a CEO of Summit HR Worldwide, an outsourcing company located in California's Silicon Valley. "Americans have, unlike Indians, an effective way to think out of the box that I would like my Indian brothers to learn," he says. "For too long we have been taught to do as we were told. It's time to think in forward tense."

Indian-born professor Abhijit Banerjee, of MIT's Sloan School of Management, who is also a personal friend of mine, observed that the strength of Americans lies in their being by and large straightforward and blunt, with little respect for formalities and rituals. He says wryly that Indians, who have centuries of Eastern customs and philosophies as their cultural and intellectual foundation, don't understand that Americans don't understand Indians at all. In his view, Americans don't grasp why the whole world doesn't see life and do business the way Americans do; their attitude is, "Why do foreigners have to be so complicated?"

So, given the gaps of communication a first-time American businessman or businesswoman may be faced with when doing business in India, here is a ready reference:

A Short List of Practical Tips
for Doing Business in India

Learn "Indian Standard Time." For North Americans, Europeans, and Japanese who are accustomed to following schedules by the clock and being punctual, the cavalier manner in which Indians treat time comes as a rude shock. An hour late for an important business meeting is no big deal, as Indians set their own time, giving Greenwich Mean Time a run for its money. One definition of Indian Standard Time is "an hour late, a day late, or never."

Have patience. Even important business meetings in India will more often than not begin with a gush of small talk—including remarks on the weather and inquiries about the welfare of your family. You could also show similar respect for your Indian counterpart's family to build a rapport. Relationships are important in the Indian context.

Think twice before offering to shake hands with a woman. Be careful about shaking hands when meeting an Indian female business colleague for the first time. Wait for the first move from her side. Although in modern business circles the trend is fast changing, until lately, out of respect for women, most men would not expect to shake hands. Instead, the custom is to offer the Indian greeting "Namaste" (nuh-MAHS-tay).

It's not just about money. Indians want to recognize the value in any business engagement, in addition to money, of course. Politeness, honesty, and sincerity will go a long way in paving the path for striking up a business deal.

Be tactful. Aggressive behavior in business dealings is frowned upon by Indians, who consider aggression in any form as a precursor to more arm-twisting in future. Smile and be polite always; adding the respectful title "ji" following the person's name will be appreciated (Vinay ji, William ji). That's a sure-shot way to win the confidence of pretty much any Indian businessman. And if you disagree with something, try not to say a straightforward no. Instead, convey the turn-down with some gentle nonverbal communication.

Offering a gift. If you take gifts for your counterparts at a meeting, make sure you offer them with both hands. Flowers, an appropriate gift in the United States when going to a friend's house for dinner, is in India appropriate with business associates as well. It's a sign of respect. Oh—and take care that the gift wrapping is not black, nor white—both colors are supposed to be inauspicious.

On the flexibility of deadlines. The Indian mind also has some difficulty with the concept of deadlines, an attitude that can be very frustrating to foreigners. Fortunately, Westerners dealing with India's high-tech, outsourcing, and biotechnology companies won't run into this problem—though being a bit late for meetings is still considered acceptable.

Address the person by their title. Indians are sticklers for flaunting their degrees. It's is a status symbol for us. So do use titles such as Doctor or Professor wherever applicable. Otherwise, a simple Mr. or Ms. will do.

Understand the Indian yes. One might expound for pages on the misunderstandings that result from the Indian "waggle"—that wobbling of head that resembles an American shake of the head, but in this case only means "OK" or "I understand what you mean."

The average Indian you may meet on the road—whether Hindu or Muslim, rich or poor, man or woman—generously peppers traditional wisdom with pragmatic nuggets of insight drawn from his or her very own experience of India. Every Indian is a delightful philosopher who lives out a life consumed by an inexplicable passion for tradition while in most cases also embracing parts of the modern matrix. The Indian way of life cannot be called "religious"; it is driven by a common love for a set of values and ideals, which at best find different expression across the diverse cultures and religious paths.

Finally, India may enchant, energize, or exhaust, but it never lacks in exuberance and effervescence. India lives forever on the frontier of change, constantly reinventing herself as she responds to imminent realities with the twin tools of her cultural tradition and spiritual wisdom.

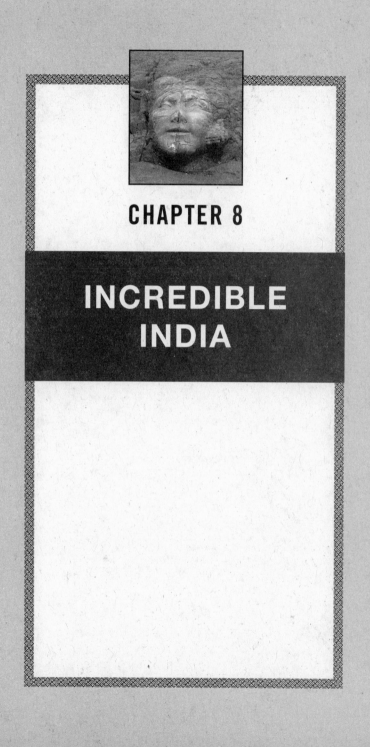

CHAPTER 8

INCREDIBLE
INDIA

When I first visited [India], I was stunned by the richness of the land, by its lush beauty and exotic architecture, by its ability to overload the senses with the pure, concentrated intensity of its colors, smells, tastes, and sounds. It was as if all my life I had been seeing the world in black and white and, when brought face-to-face with India, experienced everything re-rendered in brilliant Technicolor.
　　　　　　—Keith Bellows, Editor-in-chief, *National Geographic Traveler*

It was the late 1960s, that era of hippies, dropping out and dropping acid, and "free love." The decade throbbed to the sound of the Beatles, four young guys from the midlands of England who had become the biggest sensation in popular music the world had ever known. So when George, Paul, John, and Ringo announced they were going to take three months off their touring schedule to study yoga meditation at an ashram in India, the news that they were dropping out of sight for a while came as a shock to their fans.

Maharishi Mahesh Yogi, the founder of Transcendental Meditation who was to become the Beatles' guru, had earlier decided he could find a wealthier class of client in Europe than in India, and he traveled to England. The Beatles heard about him, visited with him in Wales, and that was enough to convince all four—each of them feeling some kind of emptiness despite all the attention and acclaim—that they would see if the sadhu's claims of inner peace through meditation could bring them satisfaction. But this wasn't an effort to pursue in Wales or England; how could anyone find peace with ten thousand screaming fans crowding the sidewalks every time they stepped outside?

Instead the Beatles traveled to India, to the sadhu's ashram (the word actually means "guesthouse") at Rishkesh, in northern India, in the foothills of the Himalayas. Maharishi Yogi gave them each a mantra and lessons in meditation, and they sat around wearing necklaces of flowers, trying to clear their minds of all distracting thoughts. And writing songs; legend says in a fiery burst of inspiration they created forty-eight new pieces. Beatle George Harrison told another ashram guest, "The meditation buzz is incredible. I get higher than I ever did with drugs. It's simple, the vibration is on the astral plane, and it's my way of connecting with God."

It was India's Technicolor canvas of peace, meditation, and spirituality that caught the imagination of the global travelers in that flower-power era—a decade remembered for protests against the Vietnam War and marches for civil rights, when free love, birth control pills, drugs, and rock-'n'-roll ruled alongside prejudice, war, and political upheaval.

The Beatles' trip spurred a generation of lost souls and seekers of inner peace who picked up the idea from them and followed them to India. Hippies came to India in droves, lured by the antimaterialistic symbols of transcendental meditation and yoga. Liberated youngsters from across the globe, girls as well as boys, flaunted their copies of the *Kama Sutra* (the illustrated love manual so ancient there is no record of when it was written), which offered discussions on kissing, foreplay, the sexual act, courtship and marriage, and courtesans, but is best known for its listing of sixty-four different positions for the sexual act.

(Still today, the *Kama Sutra* remains a popular marriage gift among Indians. In the United States, there are dozens of different editions available.)

And people like the twenty-something college dropout named Steve Jobs came too; he spent months traveling across India, barefoot and dressed like an Indian beggar, before returning home to start Apple Computer and eventually, thanks to movies like *Toy Story,* to become a billionaire.

But the sixties ended. The hippies got their hair cut, found jobs, and settled down to start families in the suburbs. They would not be going back to India anytime soon. Neither would the generation that followed them. India as a travel destination was out of the headlines. The country fell off the global tourist's radar.

The more watchful in the Delhi establishment—caught up in attending to the more pressing issues of combating poverty and education and meeting health-care needs of a rapidly growing populace—took notice of the sag in tourism and lamented it but came up with no solution. Quite the opposite: the government even took steps to discourage tourists, loading on burdensome visa restrictions that seemed to say, "Stay home." For forty years, tourism to India was down to a pathetic trickle of the audacious and the curious.

Meanwhile countries like Thailand, Malaysia, China, and Singapore surged far ahead. When you consider that tourism provides nearly eleven percent of worldwide GDP today and is "one of the world's largest industries" (so says the International Institute for Environment and Development), the lack of tourism was a big missed opportunity for the tottering Indian economy.

When its economy started taking off, India finally woke up. In 2002, the Indian Ministry of Tourism launched a massive, well-crafted campaign on a worldwide platform. Called "Incredible India," the colorful and vibrant program has for the first time in the history of the country been presenting a cohesive message of what India has to offer. And it's working.

Indeed, India's unique seven-thousand-year-old recorded history, her millions of gods and goddesses, her phenomenal diversity of cultures, landscapes, and gold-capped temples, her riot of colors and her blend of religions, have begun capturing attention in the highly competitive tourist industry.

The new tourism campaign conveys the splendor of India, showcasing the breathtaking Himalayas—the highest mountain range in the world—arid deserts, plunging rivers, verdant forests, wildlife reserves roamed by elephants, leopards, and tigers, and snug hill stations (charming retreats built by the British during the Raj as places to escape the stifling summer heat). It promotes India's vast meadows, white sand beaches, and exotic islands, along with the thousands of ancient forts, palaces, temples, and mosques, all targeted to attract the backpacker, the adventurer, the drifter, the pilgrim, the explorer, the hiker, and the die-hard romantic—as well as the business traveler and that new category called the "medical tourist."

Even sitting as far away as Europe, Canada, the United States, Australia, or the Far East, one can easily tune in to the reverberations of this now global PR campaign. The Tourism Ministry's bid is to turn the country into a popular global tourist destination. For instance, huge billboards in New York tempt tourists to try out India's Ayurvedic medicine—a school of traditional healing—as a natural stress-buster.

The government's dedication to boosting tourism is also visible in India's open-skies policy. The aviation sector has been allow to boom multifold in the last few years, tourist visas have been made easier to obtain, and tax rates in the hospitality sector have been lowered.

As late starters go, in only a few years, India's tourism campaign

Naintal, situated in the outer foothills of the Himalayas, is one of northern India's main summer tourist destinations. (*Arjun Singh*)

has managed to do more than its part in speeding up the tourist visits to the country, doubling the number of arrivals in just the first two years. In addition, the government's most recent 2006 accounting illustrates that tourism value pumped up the country's GDP by a stunning amount, more than two and a half percent.

The lure of the Incredible India campaign—some elements of which have won acclaim at global advertising award ceremonies—is continuing to produce results. Even the UN's World Tourism Organization has predicted a rosy path ahead for India's tourism sector. The campaign has gone on to become a popular case study in integrated marketing communications—with over a dozen advertising agencies working in close coordination with the Indian government.

A flurry of international airlines—British Airways, Continental Airlines, and American Airlines, among others—are stepping up their India thrust by launching daily nonstop services, with their business seats full weeks in advance.

The government of India's ad campaign is beating the drum domestically as well. Leisure time and its first cousin, the vacation—concepts not much engaged by the Indian people—are becoming an accepted part of their lifestyle, hand in hand with the rise of another Western feature: disposable income. Newly affluent Indians are exploring the beauty of their own country before venturing out to another. Thanks to India's geographical vastness, most Indians have seen little beyond their own region. Tempted by the colorful images of the campaign, domestic tourists are actively seeking out the historical, geographic, and cultural diversity of their own nation. In a country where over seventy percent of domestic travel was once restricted to religious tourism, three hundred million Indian tourists a year are now spreading their wings to see the length and breadth of their own country.

The luxury hotels popping up in India these days offer the kind of old-world charm that many people think doesn't exist anymore—even rooms with butler services, personal Jacuzzi, and sauna. The Taj Group of Hotels, the Sheraton Group, the Oberoi Group, and the Imperial, among a host of other luxury chains, have emerged as the crown jewels of India's hospitality sector.

Walk into any Taj Group hotel in India and rest assured that the hotel has serviced countless heads of state and corporate czars through the years. Visitors are greeted by a gatekeeper dressed as a noble, who bows down ceremoniously in greeting. The plush reception rooms have an authentic aura that announces, "Royalty lived here."

The Imperial Hotel, located in the heart of New Delhi, has been selected as one of the best in the world by *Condé Nast Traveler*, which also gave a world-class ranking to the hotel's Spice Route restaurant. When Chelsea Clinton dined there during a recent visit, she called the restaurant "a beautiful place with incredible food. A terrific taste of India and South Asia. . . ."

Americans think of the United States as offering diverse landscapes and attractions—from Times Square to the Statue of Liberty, the New England coastline to the warm hospitality of the Southern states, the Great Lakes region to the wilderness of the Rockies, the sunny beaches of the West Coast to the bustle and glitter of Beverly Hills and Hollywood. Diverse, indeed . . . but India answers with the, old American phrase, "You ain't seen nothin' yet."

India's Wild West: Redolent with History

The state of Rajasthan, tucked away in the northwestern reaches of the country, gives a taste of the incredible macroreality that is India. It's a virtual haven for the history buff. The region resonates with stories and visual treats of ages gone by—kings, queens, battles, intrigue, drama, love, and passion. The most visible façade of this great sense of history and romance is the palaces and forts scattered all over, many of which have now been converted into luxury hotels, where the magnificence of royal ambience fills every room and corridor.

One splendid example, the Rambagh Palace Hotel in the state capital, Jaipur, was built in 1835 by the then queen of Jaipur, to be converted into a royal hunting lodge later. The beginning of the twentieth century saw the maharaja of Jaipur residing here, and it was only in 1972 that the palace was converted into a heritage hotel. It is now a Taj Hospitality Group property. Visitors sitting in its outdoor café, soaking in the green expanse and ornate carvings on the walls, are easily transported back into the eighteenth-century aristocratic saga of the city's royal family. The authentic luxurious ambience and the regal expanse of surrounding lawns evoke images of polo-playing aristocratic kings and queens from the era gone by.

Jaipur also boasts the unexpected delight of the Hawa Mahal, the "Palace of the Breeze." Built in 1799 as part of the palace of a ma-haraja, the Hawa Mahal has an unusual exterior: though it's only five stories high, it has 953 small windows facing the street. The design had a clever dual purpose: As the housing for the maharaja's harem, the small windows allowed the young women to enjoy observing the street life of the city without being seen themselves. At the same time,

Hawa Mahal, or the "Palace of Winds," in Jaipur. Its original intention was to allow ladies of the harem to observe everyday life in the street below without being seen.   (*Hindustan Times*)

the many small openings provided a breeze (hawa) that kept the interior cool in the heat of the summer.

Not far away is the charming town of Udaipur, with its 250-year-old Lake Palace, another restored heritage hotel. Once the summer retreat of the ruling maharaja, the stunning white marble hotel sits right in the middle of an island on the Udaipur Lake, which means that hotel guests must be ferried in by boat. The royal décor and the lily pond courtyard, combined with the green mountain ranges as a backdrop, made the perfect setting for the 1980s James Bond flick *Octopussy*. The visitor to Udaipur who has seen Bond doing the cycle rickshaw stunt in the film will catch quite a few of those scene stealers here.

Throw in the desert (the dusty and colorful town of Jaisalmer), the mountains (the cozy hill station Mount Abu), the well-lit ancient forts and palaces, and a forest reserve of Ranthambore for an exciting safari, and there's a package deal going for Rajasthan that makes the most hardened traveler smile in delight.

On the streets, the visitor sees the people of this region dressed in the most vibrant reds, oranges, and pinks—even the men.

In 2000, when President Bill Clinton visited India, a highlight of the trip was his detour to a village called Nayla, near Jaipur, where he shook a leg to the rhythm of Rajasthani folk music, along with a bunch of excited rural women dressed in all their colorful finery. Clinton had come for a taste of Indian grassroots democracy, but left with pictures of the afternoon being splashed all over front pages—a major marketing coup for the state government.

The Rajasthan state government isn't the only one in India to realize the many advantages of boosting tourism as a way of moving the state up the economic ladder; the success of the Incredible India campaign is prompting many Indian states to head in a similar direction, with respective state tourism boards (or at least the richer ones) propping up their arsenals by pumping more cash into marketing their state to international and domestic tourists.

The neighboring state of Gujarat is being promoted by the local tourist board for its cultural extravaganza, branding the region as "Vibrant Gujarat: where life is a celebration." And what a place for celebrating: the state puts on some three thousand festivals and fairs every year, many of them stemming from mythology and religion. Visitors in September and October are able to take in the annual all-night dance extravaganza that draws millions of tourists every year, commemorating the divine mother goddess.

Fertile, beautiful, and prosperous, the region is the birthplace of the colorful Indian deity Krishna (yes—of the world-famous Hare Rama Hare Krishna movement, which drew the Beatles' George Harrison). Nearby Porbunder draws many history fans: it's where Gandhi was born; one local library boasts shelves crammed with Gandhian volumes.

The adventurer can take a Jeep safari at the Gir Wildlife Sanctuary—home of the majestic Asiatic lion. And for a taste of the region's cultural past, the tourist authorities will point the way to the sprawling Dwarkadhish Temple, which honors Lord Krishna. Nearby, beaches and temples dot the thousand-mile coastline. The area also abounds with buildings that look as if they might have been picked up from alongside a canal in Venice and plunked down here. Nearby Ahmedabad houses fifteenth-century mosques and countless havelis—the lavish personal residences of the rich. From here, it's not a long trip to Dholavira, an important site of the ancient Indus Valley civilization.

The business-friendly government of Gujarat offers a host of opportunities for the discerning investor; great opportunities exist in the textile, dairy, and petrochemical industries. The coastal areas also offer great potential for development, with many privately promoted ports, and new ones currently under development. Another booming area for investment in Gujarat is the food processing sector, where the government is actively soliciting overseas investment.

Outside Mumbai, the cities, towns, and regions of Maharashtra have plenty more on offer, including miles of silver-white beaches. On the other hand, lovely beaches can be found in almost any corner of the world; this region offers a treasure far more rare: the paintings and sculptures in the ancient historical caves at Ajanta and Ellora. And more examples of the India of old: sanctuaries, forts, shrines, and charming hill stations at places like Khandala, Lonavala, and Mahabaleshwar.

On the western coast of India is the "pearl of the Orient," Goa, the city that the Portuguese found so captivating. And so did Hollywood superstars Brad Pitt and Angelina Jolie—they snuck away from the set of the feature film *A Mighty Heart*, in 2006, for a quick weekend in Goa, reportedly checking into a guesthouse in Ashvem Beach. But they certainly weren't alone; Goa is visited by hundreds of thousands of foreign and domestic tourists each year, and has become one of the most popular holiday destinations for European travelers.

"Travelers discover a romantic and other-century Goa in its medieval small towns, and beautiful villages, with rich flora and fauna," advertises the Goa tourism Web site. The sunny beaches, quaint churches, gently blowing palm trees, and incredibly laid-back lifestyle right next to the water are just part of the attraction of this charming state. The streetscapes, architecture, dance, cuisine, and crafts of the region boast an all-pervasive Portuguese influence. This unique cultural confluence of East and West is a trademark of Goan lifestyle.

A face of Shiva, one of the oldest gods of Hinduism, carved into a rock on Little Vagator Beach in Goa   (*Arjun Singh*)

Northern India: of Bucolic Pleasures and Heaven on Earth

The northern Indian state of Haryana, surrounding New Delhi on three sides, is blessed with none of nature's bounties—no sea beaches, gurgling rivers, or lush mountain greenery. Not to be defeated by its lack of traditional tourist attractions, at the turn of the century the state-owned Haryana Tourism Corporation went looking for alternative options and began developing a unique farmhouse tourism concept. In partnership with local farmhouse owners, they began touting to visitors—both domestic and international—the bucolic pleasures of a distinctive village life, promoting quaint farm-land experiences like bullock cart rides, kite flying, celebrating local festivals with the rural populace, and living in mud and straw huts to indulge the nonconventional tourists with an "unforgettable slice of the countryside."

The region boasts the now globally renowned concrete jungle of Gurgaon. The towering steel-and-glass skyscrapers, sprawling malls, and bustling metropolitan environment is bound to make you feel that you've stumbled onto a different India altogether. A conducive foreign-investment climate promoted by the state government, developed and diversified infrastructure, and proximity to the national capital has made Gurgaon a hub of global business and IT players who flock here in large numbers. If India is labeled the back office of the world, Gurgaon plays a huge role in granting her that tag, with its flurry of call centers and other technology companies; together they generate nearly thirty percent of the revenues for this region. No wonder the state government has devised attractive incentives for those wishing to invest in the IT and biotech industries.

Mcleodganj, in the northern Indian state of Himachal Pradesh, as one of the closest cool getaways from New Delhi, was turned into a popular hill station. But when the British shifted their summer capital to Shimla, tourism in Mcleodganj declined tremendously. A resurgence has come since 1960, when His Holiness the Dalai Lama fled Tibet and took refuge in the upper part of the city. The region has become a haven for Buddhists globally. Cindy Crawford, Richard Gere, Christy Turlington, Steven Seagal, Pierce Brosnan, Harrison Ford . . . the list of celebrity visitors to this city is nearly endless.

The neighboring states of Uttar Pradesh and Uttaranchal offer their peculiar political history to the discerning traveler—having given a fair share of prime ministers to the country so far. Combined, the two states hold the largest population among states in India. In Uttaranchal specifically, tourism is the largest industry—and why not? The state is the proud location of the Valley of Flowers, which, due to the sheer number of plant species in its fold, is no less than a miracle of nature. In July and August, the visitor saunters through beds of flowering asters and sencios, pink and white roses, and numerous other blossoms, against a backdrop of picturesque mountains.

Not too long ago, when anyone talked about a holiday in India, it was most often a one-stop affair: to the Taj Mahal in Agra, the mausoleum of love that seventeenth-century Mogul emperor Shah Jahan, brokenhearted, built for his wife, Mumtaz, after her untimely death. No matter how many excellent photographs one has seen of this gleaming white marble structure, the magnificence of the design and the flawless quality of the workmanship are truly breathtaking.

It would be shortsighted to talk of the quaint beauty of northern India without mentioning the Kashmir Valley. The Mogul emperor Shah Jehangir, when he first laid eyes on the beautiful valley, said: "If there was heaven on earth, it is here, it is here, it is here!"

The heavenly qualities of the Kashmir Valley have been plagued by militancy for over a decade now, but things are looking up, and the state government is leading a movement to restore tourism to the region. Visitors are tempted by a peaceful glide in a native boat called a shikara on the mossy Dal Lake waters, or spending time in a gaily decorated houseboat while colorful Kashmiris dole out the best local cuisine—experiences guaranteed to create a blissful solitude.

India's East: A Cultural and Literary Feast

The "cultural capital of India"—Kolkata, the capital city of West Bengal—was until 1911 the capital of all India. The remains of its past glory are still alive in its quaint public architecture. It still is the commercial capital of eastern India and an emerging investment destination, with a familiar look to some visitors, since the Hollywood feature *City of Joy* was shot here—the story of an American doctor, played by Patrick Swayze, who wanders in search of meaning in his life.

Here's the West Bengal Tourism Board's sales pitch for attracting more visitors: "The land of exotic charms welcomes you to explore its natural treasury." Anyone who has ever dreamed of stepping into the past—a place untouched by the rush of change—owes himself a visit to the Sunderbans (it means "Beautiful Forests"), a forest swamp near Kolkata, comprised of a group of islands, many of them in such a pristine state that they don't even have electricity. In a day and age when it's tough to imagine anyplace without electric lights and television sets, this place is sure to come as a huge relief or a huge shock.

In eastern India, the state of Orissa, too, enjoys acclaim for its beaches, fine woven crafts, and the ancient yet stark temple of Konark—built in the thirteenth century and dedicated to the sun god—which takes the form of a sun's chariot, since, in ancient Hindu mythology, the sun god traveled in a chariot pulled by seven horses. Also referred to as the Black Pagoda, the temple is a world heritage site and a pleasure to behold amid the surrounding sands.

People who have visited the northeast swear that there's no place quite like it. A mix of lofty mountains, lush valleys, and dense forests, the northeast is ethnically very different from the rest of India. The area, rich in myriad dance and music forms, is the melting point of extremely large tribal populations. Assam is home to the one-horned Indian rhino. One precaution that the locals always hope visitors have heard in advance: Cherrapunji, in Meghalaya, is a place to arrive well prepared with umbrella, raincoat, and boots: it's the wettest place in the world, and monsoon is their only season!

Down South: God's Own Country

The peninsular part of the subcontinent comprising southern India is almost a different country in itself—where the landscape, language, climate, people, and even cultural traditions are quite different from those of its northern counterpart. In Tamil Nadu, the language spoken—Tamil—is among the oldest literary languages in the country. White sandy beaches warmed by the sun, coconut palms and casuarinas groves, and ancient temples bespeak a bygone age. The state tourism body aptly brands itself to domestic and international tourists as "enchanting Tamil Nadu."

Kerala, another sleepy state on the southern tip of India, is the emerging star on the tourism landscape. Exotic, fun, strikingly lovely, it's the other face of new India, the one that doesn't reside in the business districts. Life, they say, comes to a standstill at Kerala. After that, it's just placid indulgence on the limpid waters. Author Arundhati Roy captured the world that is Kerala in her Booker Prize–winning novel, *The God of Small Things*.

The largest inland water body in Kerala is Lake Vembanad, in Kuttanad, which is one of the rice bowls of the region. Also known as

"God's own country" for its scenic crisscrossing canals, and shaded by the gentle breeze under towering coconut trees, Kerala soothes the senses like no other place.

But the big attraction here, the drawing card that brings many visitors despite the weather, is Kerala's specialty in the Ayurvedic healing massages. These massages have become so popular that the Kerala Tourism Development Corporation now has a "Monsoon Rejuvenation" package for tourists, which combines sightseeing tours with the Ayurvedic treatments. And there's a massage program to fit every budget. "Ayur" means life, and the entire Ayurveda philosophy centers around the fact that the whole body should be treated—physically as well as in mind and spirit. That is why staying at the center during treatment is recommended—to purify the whole body.

A trip down to the Tirupati Temple—the second richest religious body in the world after the Vatican—pulses with a distinctive feel of its own. Tirupati is said to have been the abode of Lord Venkateshwara and is located amid the thickly wooded hills of the region. Every year millions of devotees throng the temple with gifts of gold and silver ornaments for the deities; it's said that whatever wishes one has get fulfilled here, if the residing gods are satisfied with your level of devotion. In fact, the entire town's economy relies on Tirupati's earnings—with scores of restaurants, hotels, and tour operators thriving in the region. This area also draws a great many technology workers and executives to the fast-emerging global IT hub of Hyderabad.

Here's another curious bit of native culture: In certain parts of south India, it's a usual practice for a girl to be first offered for marriage to her mother's brother. To be fair, a lot of these practices are being broken down, particularly in urban centers where the incidence of arranged marriages is getting less and less common. But the older tradition remains too—so both tradition and modernity (in the form of love marriages, where people are marrying across caste and even religious divides) exist side by side.

Caves, Rocks, and Forests Beautify Central India

Ancient peoples probably painted cave walls in many parts of the world, but few examples of their art have survived. Central India is one region where they have, attracting many who seek the unique. This region also pulses with wildlife sanctuaries and a vibrant tribal life. The states of Madhya Pradesh and Chattisgarh, defining a rough border between northern and southern India, boast several deep valleys, dense forests, many rivers, and ancient forts and palaces, as well as nearly a fifth of the country's tribal communities.

Rudyard Kipling's famous *Jungle Book* was set amid the Mahadeo Hills in the western part of the region. Kipling didn't mention another distinctive attraction that draws many: the erotic sculpture of the temples in Khajuraho. Built by followers of the tantric cult, who believed that gratification of earthly desires paved the way for emancipation, the thousand-year-old carvings in these temples contain explicit sexual motifs.

In February and March every year, millions of domestic and foreign tourists throng Khajuraho to take part in the annual dance festival, where acclaimed classical dancers and musicians perform against the stunning backdrop of the floodlit temples.

Festivals in India: A Riot of Colors and Lights . . .

Every part of the world boasts about its festivals. Some of India's will amuse and delight in their unusual extremes. Visitors who arrive in March get to witness the most interesting and unusual of festivals that the country celebrates: Holi, or the festival of colors, where from morning till noon children, youth, and the aged go about throwing colored powder and water at each other all over the streets and roads. It's best to come with a low sense of embarrassment and a willingness to laugh. When you take to the streets, watch out for those water-filled balloons being dropped from the windows all over town.

A visiting friend from New York recently described the Diwali as "almost like a cross between the Fourth of July and Christmas for us." True—the firecrackers that light up the evening sky certainly call Fourth of July celebrations to mind, while the bright and colorful lighting throughout the neighborhood is reminiscent of Christmas Eve in New York City. The local tourist board doesn't have to work very hard to promote this festival: word of mouth has already made it very popular.

India has other festivals galore, thanks to the great many religions and faiths practiced in the country—with names like Guru Nanak's Birthday, Mahavir's Birthday, Buddha Purnima, Muharram, and so on.

But India's cultural peculiarities are not only about the slew of colorful, bright, and inventive festivals that the nation celebrates. In India, society is driven, in most parts, by appearances. How you look, how you dress, how you behave, are critical travel components that have to be factored in before your trip.

Indian Hospitality

Where's the best place to stay for visitors to India? Ask the purists, and they'll invariably say that to get the true taste—and feel—of Indian hospitality, the best bet is to touch base with Indian friends and be a houseguest. There was a time when the houseguest would have a particular servant assigned who would cater to the guest's every need: special meals cooked to order; friends invited over so that they could meet the sacred guest, too, and make him feel more at home; and so on. But India is changing, not just economically but also socially. The traditional Indian joint families, housed in big spaces, are gradually shrinking in numbers. As we've seen, going nuclear is the trend, meaning that the young couple or single young man—or, these days, sometimes even the single young woman—moves out of the parents' home and into an apartment of their own. Space is at a premium, as is time. So the traveler won't as often be invited—as he might have been in times gone by—to make himself at home in the guestroom.

India is playing catch-up when it comes to hotel rooms—they're still in short supply. A December 2005 article in *The New York Times* points out that despite booming tourism, "India offers only 110,000 hotel rooms. China has ten times as many; and the United States forty times as many. The New York metropolitan region alone has about as many rooms as all of India." But things are looking up for the future, as both the government and private sector have realized that investment in hotel rooms is bound to give back increased returns in the near future. Senior Tourism Ministry officials confirm that by 2010 over 100,000 new hotel rooms are expected to open their doors across the country. For anyone in the hotel business, this is a time of great opportunity in India.

The Surprising Story of "Medical Tourism"

The phrase *medical tourism*—ten years ago the term didn't even exist—is rattling the cages of traditional Western doctors, who are seeing patients turn their backs on expensive medical procedures only to hop aboard an airplane, fly to some corner of the world, and have the medical work they need done there.

India is fast emerging as the most sought-after health tourism destination globally, both because of the quality of medical care available and the stunningly lower costs. Private investment money has been pouring in to set up five-star facilities offering world-class treatment.

It's not hard to understand why Americans are flying to India for medical care. According to various Web sites, heart surgery that costs $30,000 in the United States can be had for $6,000 in India, a $250,000 bone marrow transplant for about one-tenth that figure. No surprise, then, that medical tourism has become a multimillion dollar industry, with a hundred thousand patients pouring in annually to get treated for diseases and chronic ailments, as well as for liposuction, facelifts, and breast implants. And they come from all over: from Southeast Asia, the Middle East, Bangladesh, and Africa; and from the United States, Canada, and the United Kingdom.

Obviously the India health tourism rush is due not only to the costs and the quality of the medical care, said to be on a par with the best in the world. On top of that, at some facilities the patient is met at the airport, taken directly to the hospital, and installed in a private room featuring Internet access, television, and a DVD player. Remarkably, surgery is immediate. Some plans include a side trip to a major tourist spot, with all costs included in the price of the surgery.

A recent McKinsey and Confederation of Indian Industry study says that at its present growth rate, medical tourism alone—already a $299 million industry—may generate over $1.7 billion additional revenues for India by 2012. And guess which are the most sought-after superspecialties, apart from cardiology, neurosurgery, eye surgery, and hip and knee replacement? Alternative medicine practices like yoga and ayurveda, drawing hordes of the over-stressed.

In the "Well-Traveled" section of the popular Web site slate.com, Seth Stevenson refers to India as the "spinach of travel destinations: you may not always enjoy it, but it's probably good for you. . . . In the final reckoning, am I glad that I came here? Oh, absolutely. It's been humbling. It's been edifying. It's been, on several occasions, quite wondrous."

And why not? Bounded on three sides by water—the Indian Ocean, the Arabian Sea, and the Bay of Bengal—and sharing land boundaries with seven different nations in South Asia, India is vast, but that is only the beginning of her wondrousness. A nation of legendary splendor, an ancient history still on display, a diversity that provides new sights and experience just down the highway—put it all together and you get a sense of, "What are we waiting for?"

In the coming years, increasing numbers of visitors—tourists, businesspeople, investors, writers, researchers, and professors—will visit India. For the first-timers, in particular, it will be a richly rewarding experience.

CHAPTER 9

A TALE OF TWO INDIAS

The Challenges of
Extreme Poverty

*One India wants. The Other India hopes. One India leads. The Other
India follows.*

That headline in the nation's leading newspaper, *The Times of India*,
threw down a challenge to the country and its leaders: Start finding answers to India's most challenging problem, the plight of its
teeming 250 million poor.

The first India is charging ahead with its strategic geopolitical
partnerships, joint space missions, scientific breakthroughs, IT successes, and entrepreneurial élan, as the number of billionaires swells
and the national GDP gallops upward.

The second India trudges on, still lacking clean drinking water,
enough food, basic education, decent health care, and wholesome housing. India sparkles in areas where one might not expect but stumbles in
the basics—like the genius able to give the definition of pi to the 999th
decimal place but unable to tie her own shoes.

Today's India faces colossal internal economic and social contradictions. "Dazzling prosperity" cohabits with "dehumanizing poverty,"
to quote Congress Party president Sonia Gandhi. An alarming
twenty-two percent of the world's poor live in India, battling hunger

and disease, despite government programs that started as early as 1951 with the first Five Year Plan. Unemployed youth vacantly stare at the multinational high-rises, debt-trapped farmers contemplate suicide, a husband's demand to have his wife's female fetus aborted ignores any concept of women's rights, skeletal urchins scavenge putrid Dumpsters in back of McDonald's for scraps to stave off starvation, and extremist messengers of terror mingle with messiahs of peace.

Key social indicators—poor female and child nutrition, low participation of women in local governance and politics, lack of doctors in rural areas, unavailability of teachers in village schools, state-level disparities in social spending—raise challenges that only a devout optimist sees as solvable in less than a generation. The embarrassing and frustrating truth is that these problems continue to exist even a full half-century after Independence. Despite the nation's intellectual capital and rich natural resources, despite her economy now generating untold wealth, India's progress in addressing social issues is painfully slow.

Yet the prognosis isn't all dark. Concerted efforts are under way in all sectors of the economy. Policy makers, businesses, civil society organizations, educational institutions, are all at work in ways that give hope. But at this point we would be more than slightly delusional to expect the poorest of the poor, who suffer the most, to be cheering yet; to them, the signs of improvement are not yet convincing.

As India emerges stronger and stronger on the economic front, the two Indias must bridge some of the more pernicious gaps between them. India's leaders have this happy providence as a goal, yet never has any social effort required planning on such a gargantuan canvas.

Attacking India's Problems

Recently the country's finance minister, P. Chidambaram, gave the country plenty of reason to be happy. The highly anticipated annual budget he presented to Parliament in February 2007 tackled many issues concerning India's sustained economic growth, particularly addressing the plagues of poverty and inadequate education. A major boost in education spending cracks open the door with incentives for encouraging underprivileged children to continue schooling. The health-care funding addresses rural health plans and alternative medicines. In agriculture, farmers in the poorer districts, including many areas devastated by drought, will finally receive long-awaited help.

Addressing basic water problems, the minister described innovative ideas now being funded for creating clean drinking water. For improving hard infrastructure, the government has created special financing vehicles that will draw from the country's foreign exchange reserves to finance major projects. The budget commission, Chidambaram announced, was focusing on initiatives to curb inflation; they will also be addressing the reduction of major duties on imports of commodities and goods, which will encourage increased global trade and propel Indian companies to be more competitive globally.

But all that good news falls under the heading of the future. How are we actually faring in expediting the country's issue-solving plans? Here's a rundown of the challenges being tackled—in some cases, on an urgent footing.

Health and Food Programs

A sight that assails every visitor to India is the startling number of beggars on the streets of the cities, and entire families living with no more shelter than a makeshift tent, or, worse, sleeping on the sidewalks and in alleyways with no protection at all. For many foreigners, nothing in India is more disturbing. Sorrowful images of a poverty-stricken nation have flooded the Western mind as the dominant image of India for the greater part of the last century.

It's worth pointing out, however, that an astounding hundred million people have been lifted out of poverty since 1991. In fact, the poverty rate has declined significantly in the recent past, from forty-two percent of the population in 1990 to nineteen percent in 2007. India's heroic ability to make progress on this, its most vital social need, becomes increasingly possible with steady strides in the national GDP. Meanwhile, a large number of nongovernmental community-based organizations, corporations, and what might be called the "spiritual sector"—charitable organizations run by some of the nation's spiritual leaders—function as the government's vital tag-team partners.

The central and state governments, after caving to insistent pressure from various grassroots campaigns, are also pouring energy into a series of well-funded programs to provide low-cost housing, food-for-work programs, and clean drinking water, starting with the poorest villages.

Though free healthcare is provided for the poor in government hospitals, the facilities offered are far from satisfactory. It's difficult to claim people are being served by health care when clinic and hospital conditions are unsanitary, needed equipment isn't available, and the jaded, overworked staff is callous in their treatment of patients. But private hospitals and health-care providers are now required to reserve twenty-five percent of their beds for poor patients and also to provide free consultation. And thanks to a government immunization program that is the largest in the world, India has successfully contained polio, tuberculosis, diphtheria, polio, and measles.

One southern coastal state, Tamil Nadu, a few years ago came up with a free-lunch program, a novelty in India even though long commonplace in the United States. Providing nutritious, hot midday meals to all schoolchildren was embraced as a brilliant new idea here, especially when it came with the prospect of reducing starvation. The program led to a landmark decision by the Indian Supreme Court in 2001 directing all state governments to provide cooked meals in all government-run and government-assisted schools; in drought-affected areas, the law requires that free lunches be provided even during summer holidays. At the same time, the court ordered that workers from the lowest class, the Dalits, be given preference for the kitchen jobs created by the program. Local mothers have pitched in, taking an active role and keeping an eye out to ensure that program funds don't get diverted.

As a side benefit, the free meal is an incentive for poor parents to make sure their children get to school.

Population Control

According to the Population Reference Bureau, "India has the world's oldest population policy, having recognized rapid population growth as a serious national concern as early as 1952." From one perspective, the news is very good: according to the UN, the birth rate in India has actually been cut in half since the 1960s, from six children per woman to three. Still, the population of India is increasing by around twenty million new births a year, and twenty-eight percent of young women give birth to their first child by the age of eighteen. Among the richest one-fifth of the population, the fertility rate—the average number of children a woman will give birth to in her lifetime—has already declined to 1.8, which is below the "replacement level" at which the population has zero growth. But among the poorest one-fifth, the rate is still 3.4.

The good news, as reported by the *Economic Survey 2006–07*, is that extrapolating the success to 2026 shows that the country can anticipate a population growth of less than one percent—encouraging news in an area considered to be the root of all of India's developmental handicaps. Much of this progress goes hand in hand with India's economic growth. As Jeffrey Sachs notes in his brilliant book *The End of Poverty*, "Modern economic growth is accompanied first and foremost by urbanization. . . . the desired number of children changes remarkably as families move from rural to urban settings."

Despite a Child Marriage Restraint Act that has been on the books for seventy-five years, nearly half the weddings in India involve a child under the legal age of eighteen. In places like Rajasthan, a full-moon night in May will see infant marriages on a mass scale. Add to that the widespread ignorance of birth-control methods, and age-old notions, especially in rural areas, that more children mean more wage-earners as well as a stronger guarantee of someone to look after the parents in their old age, and you have every new pregnancy greeted with praise and cheers.

Recognizing that the burdensome rate of population growth threatens to sink progress on all fronts, the government has thrown intensive support into a pair of efforts. One aims to convince parents that having too many children hurts their chances for escaping poverty. The other promotes birth-control education—a substantial task when you consider that a significant proportion of the target audience is so completely ignorant on the subject that they don't even understand the connection between physical intimacy and pregnancy. Sex education in schools is nonexistent. One of India's former health ministers came up with a plan to offer people television sets as an alternative form of "recreation" in the evenings—bringing to mind one impoverished man who acknowledged fathering twenty-six children, offering the explanation that "the rich have other things to do."

Grassroots work of what might be called "procreation education" is now being undertaken with the help of the younger, more forward-thinking members of each village, working hand in hand with the government efforts. Adult literacy programs for the poor are also educating women so they can make better decisions about their own health and family, leading to increased employment options and therefore the door to social and political empowerment.

Education

The current system of education, with its Western style and content, was introduced and funded by the British during their years as India's self-appointed ruler, though at the time it did little but benefit the upper classes. When India achieved independence, the literacy rate was only seventeen percent. A strong and vibrant education system is fundamental to the survival and growth of any nation-state. Gandhi always lamented the death of the Gurukul, our system of traditional education that was widely practiced and dedicated to all-around human development: physical, mental, and spiritual. At the Gurukul schools, the teacher imparted knowledge of religion, scriptures, science, medicine, philosophy, history, and even war craft.

For the new knowledge-based economy, quality school education is being targeted to reach all sections of society, not just the privileged.

The government schools, however, lack both funds and initiative, and teachers are highly unionized and politicized. Moves to privatize these schools or go in for a public-private partnership are being discussed and will most likely lead higher quality and standards.

One area of concern being addressed is the traditional practice, especially prevalent in small rural villages, of pulling girls out of school early to help the mother with household duties. A government study in 2006 found that nearly half of India's women in the fifteen-to-forty-nine age bracket had never received any formal education at all.

Problems exist at the top of the academic food chain as well. Of the more than 250 government universities, few meet academic expectations. Funds provided by the government are prone to mismanagement, and the schools themselves are subject to archaic regulations. Indian universities at times teach out-of-date material, even in subjects that have quickly changing developments, such as the sciences and economics.

With the skyrocketing need for highly qualified workers in technology and other industries, government and private-sector, nongovernmental organizations (NGO) have put a high priority on improving education standards across the board. Large numbers of new primary and secondary schools are being opened in urban and rural areas. More vocational courses are being introduced to qualify finishers for immediate employment upon course completion. Some state governments have already passed laws that allow and encourage the setting up of private universities, and many more states are following suit. The central government is considering a bill that would invite the private sector to play a major role in providing new universities. Another new bill would overturn the restrictions that have prevented foreign universities from setting up campuses in India.

What's encouraging, as I see it, is that the stranglehold on education parallels the stranglehold that choked Indian businesses until fifteen years ago. The country was able to shake off the chains around the throat of business; I'm confident that we'll see education following that example.

The Plight of Women

Women, as mothers, have a place of pride in traditional Indian spiritual thought. But over the ages, especially in the villages, the reverence for women has eroded to something more along the lines of "Raise my children" and "Why isn't my dinner ready?" While men still pray to our great female goddesses such as Lakshmi, Kali, and Durga as the highest of all gods, many men don't think twice before making an abortion decision involving their wives, or pulling their daughters from school and sending them to work to support their sons' education—often forcing the girl to eke out a living as a beggar in the streets. And even though the traditional demand that a bride's family pay a dowry has been banned by law, many husbands still torture their wives in anger that no dowry was paid.

Reaching out to lift women from their traditional role of virtual slavery, other programs help women learn their rights and encourage them to seek jobs outside the home. One campaign of television ads is highlighting how important it is for girls and mothers to look after their own health, while another aims at changing the mind-set of males to allocate as much of the family budget to raising and educating their daughters as they do to their sons. In urban communities, girls and boys are more or less on an equal footing; these changing attitudes will filter down to the villages over time.

One wouldn't necessarily expect that educating a woman in her rights would have any connection with nutrition. But in families where the household income doesn't provide enough food for all, frequently it's the mother who suffers—either by voluntarily eating less in order to feed the children, or because the husband commands her to give up her food, often to feed the boys. Along with birth control education, companion programs are in place to teach women about their rights to share equally in the family food.

Updated attitudes toward empowering women have sparked efforts to help rural women start small businesses in areas such as knitting items for sale in bazaars or overseas, turning out native craft products, or cooking foods that can be sold for cash—providing the opportunity for women to supplement the family income and gain some economic and social independence while still remaining at home to care for the family. NGOs or state-sponsored groups purchase and distribute the products.

In one surprising turnaround, the law already requires that in certain local village governing councils (called panchayats), only a woman can be elected president. And as of this writing, the Indian Parliament is already debating a law that would reserve a third of all parliamentary seats for women candidates. This step would give women larger representation in parliament and be the first of its kind worldwide.

After years of sublimation, the women of India are joining this century with their heads held high; the country as a whole is leading, by example, the world's eternal struggle for balance of power between the sexes.

Infrastructure

Since economic reforms in 1991, overall improvement in infrastructure and standard of living of people in urban areas, and to some extent in the villages, has been on the upswing. But seen from another angle, the infrastructure demands of India's expanding economy now make it urgent that the country focus its energies on a massive push to bring its support systems up to Western standards.

World-class infrastructure becomes a great equalizer among nations, but for a country as far behind the curve as India, the challenges are massive enough to seem discouraging. Improvements are required both in soft infrastructure, such as better education and health care, and in the hard infrastructure of energy, roads, ports, and airports, as well as water and sewage systems, transportation, telecommunications, and a national gas grid.

What is India doing to solve its major infrastructure hurdles? Let's take a look.

Hard Infrastructure

Transport—Road, Rail, Air. Even for a country that has the largest road network in the world, with 1.8 million miles, transport remains a prime and critical concern.

Good roads and superhighways are still a dream for most of the country except for urban areas like New Delhi, Bangalore, and Mumbai—but even in those megalopolises, the sheer number of vehicles on the road is increasing so fast that improvements can barely offer much more than keeping a bad situation from becoming far worse. The ever-present fear is that conditions will deteriorate from their present state of impossible, to intolerable. With over a million new cars and nearly five million new two-wheelers added to the traffic jams each year, you can't blame an Indian motorist for despairing.

The government is targeting the capital city of New Delhi, with the largest number of vehicles per capita, to become a role model for the rest of the country. A new world-class metro system was inaugurated in 2002, and it has given the citizens a taste of modern transport, connecting far reaches of the metropolis that can take hours to travel between by car in bad traffic, but mere minutes by subway. On the first day more than one million commuters used the new service. It's estimated that when the system is complete, more than two million will use the metro daily—a welcome contrast to the dilapidated and overcrowded New Delhi buses.

For intercity traffic, at least, some relief is promised by a twenty-thousand-mile national superhighway system currently being built. New road projects are being started by state governments as well, but attracting private capital to this lower-return investment remains a major stumbling block.

While the routes to and from India have become one of the busiest

Even on the newly constructed highway between Agra and Jaipur, camel transport is allowed. (*Emily Haynes*)

and most profitable for the big European airlines, domestic air traffic has also been growing almost exponentially since about 2000, with fares falling drastically. New airlines have taken wing, and new private airports are being built for four metro markets. Expansion of the top twenty airports is under way, but airports and the current infrastructure are as yet inadequate to handle the increased traffic, resulting in delays paralleling the slowdowns and gridlock that is the day-to-day reality of road and highway travel.

Railways remain a very important link for the masses and fortunately are now setting new standards in performance that bring smiles from satisfied passengers and commercial shippers. The maverick railway minister, Lalu Prasad, never fails to surprise with his "Lalunomics," delivering more value for every passenger rupee from the formerly in-the-red Indian Railways. Surprisingly, his tough stands have turned around the economics of this, the world's largest railway system, which now shows a revenue surplus of more than $4 billion. The trains and facilities continue to be upgraded at the same time that prices are being lowered. I personally took a train from New Delhi to the foothills of the Himalayas and my journey was pure ecstasy compared to a decade ago.

Housing. Despite the poverty figures cited earlier that show India making progress in the struggle to lift the poorest out of poverty, too many still belong to the hordes of the forgotten, living with the most meager of shelter or no shelter at all. Even if housing projects had been started a decade or two ago, the discouraging birth rate among the poor would still have made housing one of the major challenges.

Now that a conscience-stricken nation has found the will to attack the problem, difficulties such as regulations from an earlier era (rent control rules, for example) stand in the way, and the effort to knock

Slums in central Mumbai. Around forty-three percent of the population of
the city lives in shantytowns and slums.   (*Hindustan Times*)

down these barriers can be frustratingly difficult. Providing even minimal housing to slum dwellers, though heralded as a government priority, still lacks a concentrated political will. Old ways die hard.

Communications. Telephone service and the Internet can serve as
great equalizers for the poor. India's progress in electronically wiring
the nation—even bringing service to the rural hinterlands—can certainly be named as one of its great success stories.

Of course, the blessings of the telephone and Internet haven't
reached the entire country yet. But the government has set up a universal service fund that helps cover the costs of service providers—
both to continue bringing the digital age to the villages, and to
supplement the costs of keeping the electrons flowing.

Energy. You might think that a nation in which twenty percent of
the people live below the poverty level would be a small consumer of

energy. Quite the opposite: India is the world's sixth largest energy consumer.

Population growth, coupled with continued economic growth, is driving energy demand to levels above the country's production capacity. Overall, India's need for power is growing at a remarkable rate. The country's projected increase in electricity consumption is the highest for any major country.

New technology-based businesses and the multitude of product-related businesses that serve them are all responsible for the mega-use of energy. Add to that the energy used to serve all workers who spend their newfound lavish salaries on, among other conveniences, air conditioners that they run wide open for a minimum of ten months a year. Another contributing factor to the national energy drain is the fact that new commercial and business centers are in full operational status around the clock seven days a week, becoming energy gluttons.

Even in New Delhi, the nation's capital, the lights can go out and computer screens flicker off at any time of day or night. And naturally the blackouts and brownouts are much more prevalent in the heat of the summer. Electricity supply has doubled since 1991, but power generation and distribution are still largely owned and controlled by the state. Poor distribution and maintenance, along with the theft of electricity by people tapping into the lines and overunionization of the workforce, add to these power woes.

The problem has brought a bright smile to one segment of the economy: the makers and distributors of emergency generator sets. These private generators, which run on kerosene, gasoline, or diesel fuel, kick in whenever the local power grid fails. So in businesses, manufacturing plants, and the better homes and apartment buildings, when electricity stops flowing down the government's power lines, the thousands of individual generator sets kick in; lights dim for a moment and come up again. Also on the positive side, most of India's half million or so rural villages now have electricity, with only about eighty thousand remaining completely without any connection to the power grid.

Currently most of India's electricity is generated from fossil fuels, mainly coal. India is the third largest coal-consuming country in the world and that accounts for the fact that this country is responsible for half the world's total fossil-fuel-related carbon dioxide emissions. Since 1990, India's carbon emissions have increased by over sixty percent, and they are about nine times higher than they were in 1960. Much of this increase is due to India's growing use of coal for power generation.

As in the United States and other highly industrialized countries known for their traditional car-adoration mania, eyes are now shifting to energy sources that can take the place of the fossil fuels that pose the now-recognized threat of global warming.

India, blessed by being "sun-rich," is happily pursuing plans to tap the sun's energy. These plans are especially appropriate for the vast lands under the plow that require power mostly in daytime. Thankfully, harvesting of solar energy on a large scale is now commercially viable. In places like the chilly heights of Ladakh, in Kashmir, solar energy is already supplying light as well as energy for heating homes and commercial premises.

Residents and businesses along India's five thousand miles of coastline are looking to the invisible power of the wind. Even government officials were delighted to learn in early 2007 that the country has emerged as one of the fastest-growing wind-energy producers, behind only Germany, Spain, the United States, and Denmark.

With the India-U.S. rapprochement that has opened the door to Indian nuclear plants, planners are already looking to the day when the first of the new generation of plants will be going online.

Soft Infrastructure

Newcomers to the sport of "Let's Fix India" might be prepared to hit the showers at this point, feeling that the essentials have already been examined. The to-do list is, however, a good deal longer: some of the so-called soft infrastructure items are equally as important as the more tangible hard items. Here's a look at three of the most urgent soft infrastructure concerns.

Governance. This heading brings us back to the topic of the miserable salaries for public employees, with pay packets so thin that bribe-taking and corruption is a practical necessity just to put food on the table. Indians, even government employees, are quick to acknowledge that as much as twenty percent of the budget for any program is being siphoned off by sticky-fingered officials. As mentioned earlier, no one denies that the salary structure is one of the underlying reasons why so many urgently needed programs do so little good: the money is not reaching the intended destination.

Corruption aside, the Indian government is also plagued by a monumental case of over-the-top inefficiency, made worse by a mountain of archaic regulations left over from the "License Raj" that dominated Indian governance before 1991. But the revamping of bureaucracy is under way. The training of bureaucrats at the Kennedy School at Harvard and at the Indian Institute of Management in Ahmedabad in good governance, political economy, and analysis will result in giant strides forward.

At the same time, greater involvement of the private sector (through public/private partnerships) in areas ordinarily reserved for the state—electricity and public infrastructure, for example—is generating greater transparency and efficiency in planning, implementation, and use of resources.

Judicial and Legal Reforms. India has some of the world's best rules and laws, applied to real-world pragmatic legal contexts by a fiercely independent and proactive judiciary. But the virtues are sometimes hard to see when justice creaks along at a painfully slow pace. Like the Chancery Court case of Jarndyce and Jarndyce in Charles Dickens's *Bleak House,* cases in the Indian courts sometimes drag on for many years, on occasion as long as a decade or two. Today, millions of cases jam the courts.

Part of the problem lies in a system that allows appeals, even in mundane cases, through three tiers, all the way to the Supreme Court.

Criminal cases are too often filed vindictively as a way of harassing someone or seeking vengeance. Seventy percent of the jail population are prisoners awaiting trial, many of them already held for longer than the maximum sentences prescribed for their crimes.

Even if they are not jailed in the interim, the cases of those accused may not come to trial for years, and they must make continual court appearances, disrupting their ability to earn a living. Some cases are so extreme that they're almost laughable, like one action filed against ex–Miss World Aishwarya Rai, who offended someone's sensibilities by playing a role in which she was seen on-screen allowing a man to kiss her. To an American, the charge seems frivolous, yet it has been filed with the courts and is ploddingly winding its way through the justice system. One small minisolution to the deep and far-reaching legal-system problems has been the creation of some fast-track courts set up for handling consumer grievances.

Vote-Bank Politics. A popular worldwide blood sport practiced in India with an extra punch of vengeance is political power grabbing. Here vested interest groups, employing divisive politics and unethical tactics, first create and then puppeteer different pressure groups, mostly by cashing in on lurking prejudices of caste divides and differences of religion and practices—premeditatedly increasing religious bigotry in an otherwise tolerant nation.

Appealing to the prejudices of one narrow set of voters—Muslims, Dalits, or Brahmins, for example—has unfortunately become the new political art form in India. Any of these blocs of voters, referred to as a "vote bank," is manipulated to gain an upper hand. One former prime minister, V. P. Singh, achieved a low point with this manipulative tactic when he shepherded a bill through parliament—a bill for reserving up to thirty percent of all government posts for the lower castes.

Class Bias. In a society where class determines everything about one's place and role in life, the goal of moving to a society blind to class issues has more than a few stumbling blocks to cope with. No nation can legislate an end to class bias. While the police readily act upon a complaint of abuse received from a finely dressed lady speaking fluent English, a similar complaint from her slum-dwelling counterpart only ends up in the wastepaper basket. Sadly, this class bias pervades modern Indian society at all levels. As the next generation uses education to lift India out of the dark ages of repressive thought, these insults to equal rights will hopefully be eradicated from the national mind-set.

Roadblock: The Specter of Corruption

In a country where the exchange of gifts is part of tradition, it's not so easy to recognize when segments of the culture become corrupt.

Even when you're not supposed to pay for a service, such as to the postman delivering to your doorstep, you'll gladly oblige when he asks for his Diwali (festival) "bonus," and not think of him as corrupt. On the other hand, when you notice a taxi driver stopping in the middle of the night, depositing the wandering, lost-looking hippie at his budget hotel in a far corner of New Delhi and not even asking for the fee shown on the meter, you wouldn't call him "nice." You'd say he did his duty as a human.

Indians see corruption of public employees in a decidedly different light than a Westerner would. Mostly for political reasons, the country's president and prime minister are paid minuscule salaries, about two thousand dollars a month. It would be stepping on toes if any government employee, or the employee of any organization heavily funded by the government, were paid more than the nation's leaders. Scale those salaries down through all the levels of an overweight bureaucracy, and by the time you get to the bureaucrat who approves a passport application, the neighborhood letter carrier, and the constable directing traffic, the take-home pay isn't enough to live on.

Why not rescale the salaries of the president and PM to an appropriate level? Because politicians believe the move would be extremely unpopular with the huge mass of the poorest of the poor; though many of them are illiterate, India's poor are still knowledgeable about public issues, and they vote.

For the time being, at least, we are stuck with a system that pays government workers a pittance. That's not an excuse or a justification, just a way of life that Indians don't much like but have long accepted.

I'm reminded of a young cousin of mine who finished her schooling at MIT (my own alma mater) and returned to India, settling into a posh house she owned. She found her electricity was going out several times a day. I told her the solution: Pay the lines person from the state-owned electricity supply company ten dollars per month as a "sweetener," and she would have far fewer power problems. My cousin insisted it was her democratic right to have reliable power without having to pay a bribe, even a bribe she could easily afford.

As a member of my family, my cousin knew many people at high levels in the government and got in touch with the chief minister, who referred her to the chairman of the electric company. The chairman listened to her complaint and was sympathetic, but then wanted to know, "How much is the guy asking for?"

When my cousin said it was the equivalent of ten dollars, the chairman said, "I can write a complaint and get the person shifted to another position." But then he added, "You know, these guys get paid very little, and our rules and finances don't allow us to pay them any more. He isn't asking for very much. It would be better if you just pay."

The chairman of the company accepted the bribe taking and condoned it. My cousin started paying and the problems of frequent blackouts magically disappeared. We label it corruption, and it annoys us, but we also understand that it does translate to a simple way to bolster India's eternally inadequate pay scales.

Moreover, as laws and rules are in a state of flux given the dynamics of growth, some "corrupt" practices are being given the green light. As one example, under the earlier Foreign Exchange Regulations Act (FERA)—drawn up before today's economic boom—you could have been arrested for having a small stash of U.S. money in your house or office, or for going on a trip abroad with cash for daily expenses but failing to declare that a colleague had paid for one of your dinners. Virtually anyone of any position or status was guilty of these "crimes" and could have been prosecuted at any time; you routinely paid bribes to avoid prosecution. Today most of the restrictive

FERA regulations have been scrapped and the government actually encourages the use of foreign currency.

If the idea of paying petty bribes doesn't make Indians angry, the same is not true of corruption on the grand scale, such as officials siphoning off money designated for public projects, which unfortunately is not that uncommon. One former prime minister reported to the country that out of every hundred rupees of government money intended for helping the poor, typically *eighty-five* rupees goes into the pockets of corrupt officials.

Businesses and real estate developers regularly get favors from politicians and bureaucrats. Fortunately, stories of officials with their hands deep in the proverbial cookie jar make juicy television news, and India's television stations are delighted to play detective by staging frequent sting operations and showing pictures of officials being caught and led away in shame by the constables. The motive of the airing of illicit activities may be entirely based on building audience ratings, but these reports are making sticky-fingered officials think twice about their crimes, as they watch high-profile public figures appear with increasing regularity on the evening news.

The extent of corruption differs from state to state and is closely tied to the average education level locally. The state of Kerala in the southwestern tip of the country, with the highest literacy rate, has the least corruption. Bihar, tucked up in the nation's north on the border with Nepal, has the lowest literacy (with a per capita income reported to be ninety-four dollars per year), and tops the corruption list, with many elected officials on the bad-guys list.

Individual citizens are joining the crusade of ethical standards. A quiet public servant with the Indian Revenue Service, Arvind Kejriwal, quit his job to devote himself to a single issue: He recognized that little headway could be made in mopping up the slime of corruption as long as the government continued to hide reports of its activities behind a veil of secrecy. He spearheaded an intensive campaign that actually brought about the passage of new legislation, the Right to Information Act, which allows private citizens to demand and obtain government documents revealing financial and other details of public programs. Kejriwal has been hailed for "empowering the poorest citizens of India's capital city to fight corruption."

Since passage of the bill in 2005, private citizens have been uncovering previously well-hidden examples of officials dipping into the public till. State agencies, spurred by these efforts, have been cracking down, and the media has been eagerly training their spotlights on catching greedy officials and congressmen accepting bribes.

Who Will Lead the Way?

No democracy can be effective unless the people take an active role in their own governance. In India, civic engagement is finally becoming a reality, with important public decisions no longer being made behind closed doors but instead within full view of the public. Elite members of society—particularly the well-educated and university scholars—are becoming increasingly vocal, launching public discussions and debates that stir taxpayers into a greater awareness and potential involvement in the most pressing issues, and their possible solutions, facing Indian society.

Still, India's academics lag well behind their counterparts in the West when it comes to leading debate on critical public policy issues. I believe that the privatizing of the university system would serve to build academia's interest in participating in the public issue forum.

Some progressive state governments are, however, leading open debates on greater public participation in the reforms process. In 2003, the state of Karnataka legislated periodic interface between local civic bodies and citizens on several policy matters. This legislation is an excellent precedent, which has also been followed by some other states to create platforms for dialogue.

Despite an awkward title that defines a group by saying what it isn't, the nongovernmental organizations, or NGOs, are performing the admirable task of dealing with all kinds of issues and helping the poor where the state seems to be lagging. India's NGOs range from groups such as Barefoot College—which trains poor villagers to install solar panels and hand pumps—to teams of doctors whose mobile medical units travel to villages offering vaccinations and treatment for ailments from malaria to HIV.

These groups, unfortunately, rarely work in a unified way—not by combining forces with other NGOs, nor by teaming up with a government agency. But one thing is for sure: NGOs have immeasurably helped bring clean water, housing, health care, renewable energy resources, and more to India's poor. One NGO, Ruchika, devised an ingenious approach for getting some brand-new concepts into the heads of prematurely hardened kids who were forced by life circumstance to hit the streets to earn money for their families instead of sitting in classrooms. And the solution had nothing to do with subsidizing the families.

One particular group of young boys earned money on the railway platforms of their city—shining shoes and running errands for passengers waiting for the next trains. Ruchika actually set up schools in the railway station. When a train came in, the boys stood at the ready to make whatever money they could. As soon as the train left, they return to their studies in math, science, and other standard subjects. After another "work break" it was back to the books.

Like NGOs, many of India's businesses are showing a sense of social responsibility. It's my experience that most businesspeople have a caring heart and don't mind doing what they can to help the underprivileged.

The corporate sector is an important and wealthy stakeholder in the twin issues of alleviating poverty and illiteracy. Corporations could and must do a lot more, especially as they are currently leading India's wealth creation. The concept of passing down wealth from father to son as a matter of duty to the family name, standard in America, to a large extent slows down a wealthy person's ability to give more to charity. However, attitudes are changing among the Indian wealthy. The experience of the IT sector, where newcomers, with just their entrepreneurship, made it big without business godfathers or government contacts, is a case in point. This generation is now infusing businesses with a new conscience. Bulky organizations with hierarchical setups and sundry relatives are getting leaner and flatter, with meritocracy being the new buzzword. Leadership is inspiring employees by exemplary conduct. For example, when Azim Premji's son was relocating from New York to London and wanted to reside in the company guesthouse for a few days, he was flatly refused: the guesthouse is for employees and customers, not for family.

Reasons for Hope

The two Indias: One has its face turned upward, savoring the warmth of sunshine, radiant in its newfound health; the other remains sadly staring down at the parched earth.

In its full-steam-ahead pace, India needs to seek national solidarity to achieve, in the words of our prime minister, "equity in growth—equity across regions, states, sections of society and gender, [for] we cannot walk boldly into the future with only one half of our nation shining."

Despite her massive problems, India is aggressively paving its roads to the future. Women are being offered education, accepting their rights, being educated in family planning, and, with new laws, beginning to be guaranteed a leadership role in political life and policy making. The declining birth rate promises to reduce the number of the poorest, while the rising national GDP insures that greater funding will continue to be available for addressing the most severe of India's social problems.

Government programs already under way include the building of low-cost housing, providing ample clean drinking water, and supplying jobs; in a break from the past, all improvements will start with the poorest villages. Private hospitals, acting under federal edict, are giving health care and reserving bed space for the patients who are at the lowest rungs of the social ladder. The free-lunch program, spreading rapidly across India, will both fight starvation and entice hungry children into classrooms to learn.

India's roads are being developed, with a new national highway under construction that will inspire road improvements throughout the country—though the growing population of cars will continue to make traffic jams a way of life.

And a final item on this short list that could be much, much longer—attacks on corruption will continue to increase the proportion of federal program funds that reach their destination instead of being siphoned off.

Let no one say, "Never the twain shall meet." We need to hope and expect that the people of the second India, the impoverished one, will gradually gain ground, sharing more and more with India's affluent. No wealth or position or status in the world is worth anything if we as a nation fail to take our entire populace along the path of progress.

India, often referred to as the awakening giant, while poised to play a leading role on the world stage, must at the same time face and fight its problems at home. This campaign for self-improvement will be helped by a surging economy and a vibrant democracy.

A cynical definition says that an optimist is a person who doesn't understand the problems. I believe that anyone awake to what's taking place in India today can see the problems, and still be an optimist.

And that encouraging verity is very new in India.

CHAPTER 10

THE INDIAN CENTURY

If I were asked under what sky the human mind has most fully developed some of its choicest gifts, has most deeply pondered on the greatest problems of life, and has found solutions, I should point to India.

—Max Müller

India was the mother of our race and Sanskrit the mother of Europe's languages. She was the mother of our philosophy, mother through the Arabs, of much of our mathematics, mother through Buddha, of the ideals embodied in Christianity, mother through village communities of self-government and democracy. Mother India is in many ways the mother of us all.

—Will Durant, historian and author

India earned its "golden bird" label centuries ago because of her inexhaustible riches and enviable advantages in trade and commerce, which paved the way for her twenty-four-percent share of world trade in the seventeen hundreds. England, as conqueror, sucked out India's leadership as a key innovator in science, agriculture, industry, and technology. And India's profound spiritual heritage has spread the world over, with Buddhism in particular taking root throughout Southeast Asia, Japan, and China.

Life and times, it seems, have uncannily come full circle. Sixty years after shrugging off the British yoke, Indians are finally emerging from the mind-set of a dominated people, staking claim to their rightful place in the modern global village. With an economic growth rate confidently surging ahead at a near double-digit rate, spurred by an innovative, well-educated young working population on the move, nurtured by the country's scientific prowess, entrepreneurial spirit, and vast natural resources, all built upon a high sense of spiritual strength, you can understand why the word *superpower* comes to mind.

The center of gravity of world power and international focus can now be seen to be slowly but surely shifting from the Euro-Atlantic region to Asia. India, often referred to as the "awakening giant," is, with its surging economy and vibrant democracy, poised to play a leading role on the world stage.

No wonder Indians are exuding confidence once again. The country's entrepreneurs are today moving beyond providing low-end IT services to take leadership in the most complex arenas of technology and biotechnology. While Silicon Valley and the world's other technology centers continue to hire brilliant Indian techies, the newly prosperous Indian IT majors are turning the tables—making themselves better positioned to serve the global marketplace by hiring employees from the international markets they serve and buying up companies in the countries where their customers are.

Further testimony to India's knowledge edge is her growing global acclaim in research and development expertise, the reason that more than 125 Fortune 500 companies—especially global biotech and pharmaceutical majors—have opted to set up installations in India in the race for cutting-edge R & D.

What's more, the complaints frequently heard in the United States about the damage being done to the American workforce by offshoring are apparently misplaced. A 2004 study by the McKinsey Global Institute, reported in an *International Herald Tribune* article, found that offshoring actually brings considerable benefits to the American economy. Reporter Dana Farrell wrote that the practice "frees U.S. resources for activities with more value added," which allows firms to "pass cost savings on to consumers through lower prices and to investors through higher profits." While the process is inevitably damaging to many workers, overall "the U.S. economy redeploys workers who lose their jobs from offshoring in ways that boost growth as well."

India's intellectual capital is spreading like a wave around the entire world—an Indian diaspora twenty-two million strong in America, Europe, Australia, Asia, and Africa is making its presence felt from business to academia. The best of them are being hailed as global CEOs, IT head honchos, and pioneering entrepreneurs, such as Indira Nooyi of Pepsi, and Vinod Khosla, who cofounded Sun Microsystems.

Like their forefathers in ancient India, modern Indian entrepreneurs are making their mark on the globe—this time in part by acquiring companies in Western markets as much as five times their size.

It's always reassuring when personal contacts who visit India for the first time form an impression that confirms all the statistical data (as well as my own beliefs). At an early stage of developing this book, the publisher of Plume, Trena Keating, came for meetings, along with her husband. Afterward she wrote me, "David and I were just talking about India and how we're crazy not to somehow invest in the country, given what you showed us. That trip sure changed our perspective on the world, in more ways than we ever could have imagined. We're both still processing what we saw and learned, and the experience only grows richer with time."

Will India Forge Ahead of China?

Review the story painted in these pages and I believe the conclusions are inevitable. While the Chinese state is making an all-out effort to conquer the IT and outsourcing arenas, and is making headway. But India remains a chief competitor because of her inherent strengths: English language skills, IT and management education, and hands-on experience since the earliest days of the age of personal computing. Global management consulting firm A.T. Kearney's 2005 ranking of the most attractive offshoring locations places India at the very top of the list, with China in second place. But according to the report, China is so far behind India that the gap between them is "larger than the gap between the next nine countries combined."

Beyond the arenas of IT and outsourcing, where India is the clear winner, the arena of high-end manufacturing is also being dominated by India. In sectors as diverse as automobile manufacturing and auto parts, telecom, hardware, engineering goods, steel, packaging, even fashion and jewelry, India is emerging as a competitive manufacturing hub. Delhi's emphasis on creating more and more Special Economic Zones for manufacturing across the country is further boosting the country's manufacturing boom.

The soaring innovative streak and driving entrepreneurial spirit of the Indian people are key ingredients cheering India to the finish line ahead of China. In contrast, the authoritative Chinese regime may be in a position to command that a factory increase their production but cannot command them to "innovate better."

Little surprise, then, that India has already edged ahead of China in crucial factors. The latest World Economic Forum's *Global Competitiveness Survey* for 2006–07 shows India at forty-third, well up the ladder compared to China, in fifty-fourth (and even further ahead of Russia and Brazil). Efficient capital markets, quality of public institutions, and a sound judicial system, among other factors, accounted for India besting her competitors.

And then add the fact that India, unlike China, is a really noisy democracy, with a vibrant civil society and vigilant media digging for the facts underlying any government claim—publicly exposing propaganda and applauding truth—and you remember again the advantages of a free and demanding press.

India's greatest weaknesses are its poor quality of universal modern education outside the sciences and its shortcomings in infrastructure and governance. China's principal weaknesses are its massive misallocation of capital by state-owned enterprises, and its government-owned banking system that allocates funds on directives rather than on sound banking practices.

A global CEO jet-setting to Shanghai would probably not notice this lack of soft infrastructure in China and would instead be wowed by the modern, glowing ports, highways, and airports; nor would he worry unduly about how China is manipulating the yuan to its trade advantage.

India's other strengths are its entrepreneurship, the global perspective of its leaders and managers, and its ability to manage complex global businesses, thanks to several generations of Western-trained elite.

In their defense, China's strong points are currently their abundant access to capital and their healthy blend of good universal education. Allowing a small crack in the wall of Communism's absolute control over all aspects of life and business, the Chinese government has opened a small degree of private ownership of companies (the richest person in the country is a woman whose company recycles paper), but full freedom is not even on the drawing board.

Former *Economist* editor Bill Emmott believes, as I do, that India has an advantage, since it is not plagued by any major internal issues of stability or ethnic disputes beyond the challenge of inclusive growth that reaches out to the country's poor. Our philosophy of destiny and acceptance of our lot as "God's wish" is a major stabilizing influence, and one that will give the country the time it desperately needs to fix its problems of equity for all.

The glowing economic projections for China completely miss out on the political and societal stability issues—how the rising wealthy population in China will react to their growing urge for political freedom and fundamental rights, how the lack of inclusiveness of the rural population in growth will affect China. Political history has shown that repressive authoritarian governments have always tumbled in time. The former Soviet Union is a clear example of a system breaking down under the forces of a call for freedom by its people. In China, I firmly believe history will unfold in the same way. India, allowing its citizens full freedom and the right to criticize the government, has never had any such revolutions or uprisings.

Even without an uprising, the dissatisfactions and unrest with a form of government that denies its citizens a voice will forever threaten continued economic progress. Yes, China is far ahead of India today, but I am convinced that the dichotomy inherent in the Chinese system—wealth creation through authoritarian discipline and centralized decision-making, versus a democratic participation of the citizens—is creating a huge disconnect. The more wealth people accumulate, the more they want freedom of action and freedom of speech.

China's long-term geopolitical goals make seasoned diplomats twitch. Bill Emmott confirms that there is a very serious concern in the United States and Europe about the long-term aims of China.

"The Chinese strongly believe that they have a Manifest Destiny to be the superpower of the world," Emmott said, adding that other nations see this belief as a danger signal. Even more worrisome is Emmott's assessment that the Chinese government would be willing to go to any extent to achieve this destiny, as they have done in invading Tibet, taking their uncompromising stand on reclaiming Hong Kong, and saber-rattling over their designs on Taiwan.

Emmott also subscribes to the strong conviction that the United States has clearly become a supporter of India's growing strength, of her standing as a benevolent power in Asia and a stabilizing influence across the world—as a government that will take the same stance as the United States in protecting sovereign nations against dictatorships and any nation or group that chooses terrorism as a weapon. Even Japan is now pushing for India's growth as a superpower, as a major balancing force to Japan's natural enemy, China. Israel similarly is backing India as a stabilizing influence in the face of the ever-present reality of Islamic terror attacks and larger threats.

The former ambassador of China to the United States, Hu Shih, has said, "India conquered and dominated China culturally for twenty centuries [through Buddhism] without ever having to send a single soldier across her border." What India achieved through religion ages ago may yet come true again, only this time through stronger economic opportunity.

India—Toward Economic Superpower and Beyond

Rarely in the history of the world has any nation ever risen economically as rapidly as India has over the past few decades. The young movers of Bangalore, and to an even greater extent Mumbai, are reveling in their professional and financial success. And they've turned to showing off their success the same way so many successful young professionals in New York and Silicon Valley do: by spending lavishly on hot cars, designer clothing, jewel-encrusted wristwatches, nights out making the rounds of the clubs, and vacations abroad. The air of energy and excitement and the frantic pulse and pace of the affluent is mind-boggling.

Yes, India has problems. But there is not even the slightest doubt in my mind whether the two Indias will merge; it is inevitable. I'm more focused on how quickly it will happen. Indians from all walks of life will concur with me—each of us is influenced by our inclusive philosophy that says "happiness for all," that no amount of economic prosperity or geopolitical successes is of value if India is unable to deliver education, health, and employment to all of our people—the poorest as well as the richest. As a businessman turned philosopher, I daily recall the words of our Vedanta prayer that says, "Let the whole world and its living beings be happy and at peace with themselves." I see an underlining vision of Indians working together to create one world, not just on the economic front but in body, mind, and spirit, to addresses the happiness, well-being, and peace of all mankind.

The Goldman Sachs analysis that puts the United States in third place economically by 2050, behind India and China, while it seems so unlikely to many, seems more logical when you recognize that the brightest twenty-five percent of the Indian population outnumber the entire population of the United States. Will the same still be true in 2050? You bet—do the math.

And how do you beat a nation like India, whose people are constantly driven by a fierce passion for life, for work, for creation, and for dreaming that brings out the best in them in a free and open environment?

When the facts are marshaled and examined, I believe the conclusion is inevitable: By 2050—in partnership with the United States and other nations—India will lead the free-world markets.

AFTERWORD

My personal life changed dramatically a few years ago, in ways that many would see as calamitous but that I clearly see as providential.

To recap a bit of my history mentioned earlier in these pages, I come from a business family and community. As such I have personal links and family relationships with most of the top old business families in India, especially the powerful and well-connected Marwaris, a long-established business community known for their keen business acumen.

My father started from small beginnings in 1946 and built several businesses to an overall cash flow on the order of a million dollars by the early seventies. When I joined the family business after my education in the United States, I expanded and diversified the business enormously into steel production, computers and IT, mobile telecommunications, engineering, financial services, hotels, and more.

Businesspeople of India remember well the difficult days when the economy was completely controlled by the government and one had to seek a license for anything one produced, every dollar one spent to import raw materials and machinery. Those were times when businesses had to bow to government dictates and even to government

tyranny—when you had to sit for days outside government-owned
banks and financial institutions to beg for loans and outside the industry and commerce ministries to beg for licenses, and might at any
time be slapped with meaningless lawsuit to harass and prosecute you
if you did not toe the line.

My journey from where I started in 1972 was a difficult one, as it was
for so many others, though my penchant for taking risks and challenging powerful forces turned business into an exciting roller-coaster ride
for me. I spent nearly thirty years growing the family business and by
1999 it reached such heights that I was listed among the top five richest
people in India and appeared in the *Forbes* magazine listing of the two
hundred wealthiest people in the world. In those thirty years I did my
best with complete dedication and focus and gave it my best shot. God
was kind.

In 2000, listening only to my inner conscience, I did what few would
have advised as good business sense: I challenged the then established
practices of business. My actions stirred up some powerful forces within
and outside the government and resulted in my being slapped with tax
and revenue inquiries, and official harassment, leading to the government filing charges against me. The main accusation was that the group
of companies of which I was chairman advanced money that was borrowed from banks to its subsidiaries and other group companies. This
practice of advancing funds within group companies—even funds borrowed from banks—was commonplace in most business groups and
known to the banks themselves. But as chairman, I was accused of having fiduciary responsibility for the so-called financial indiscipline.

This came just as the high-tech "bubble" burst in 2000 and 2001,
putting our companies under severe financial strain; the legal charges
added critically to our problems. Our access to much-needed capital was

completely eroded, leaving our companies no longer able to withstand the recession and financial strain in sectors like steel; some of the companies crashed, others I was forced to close. But I had no regrets. I had taken a stand that my conscience directed me to take. To an Indian, this can mean being driven by one's understanding of his own Destiny, his own Karma—a personal interpretation of what is right and what is wrong.

It may take a long time before my name finally gets cleared. And I'm by no means alone; many other businessmen have charges of various kinds pending against them that, legitimate or not, will be hanging over their heads, but we all learn to treat it as part of life.

I moved on in 2001, at the behest of my guru and guide, to where my true heart was: into education, into working with young minds and changing and guiding talented young people as they move forward to take on the world.

In 2002, I set up the Rai Foundation and under that umbrella launched an educational institution that now has some eight thousand students on fourteen campuses across India and will soon open campuses in the Middle East and Africa. With the encouragement of my wife, I have created a unique effort to improve the education of young women through a program we call "Girl Genius and Gifted Girl," which provides that any number of orphan girls, and three hundred girls from the poorest families, are accepted every year to receive totally free higher education, including housing and food, and an ample clothing allowance, continuing, for those qualified, to a Ph.D. These are the potential stars of tomorrow and to see them flower is pure joy. I would not trade that for any wealth. The Rai Foundation offers courses in over twenty different fields. Its many other arms address issues ranging from our ancient arts and culture, to child care, to women's empowerment, to health, with the goal of lifting people from the slave mind-sets of the past.

My business life has been a great learning curve with tremendous ups and downs, challenges, and explosive moments of happiness and despair, of meeting people from across the globe and understanding different points of view. One day perhaps I will write my autobiography, but today it's enough for me to understand and appreciate the rapid, mind-boggling pace of almost every part of an Indian's life, whether business, culture, or the environment. It's thrilling for me to be an intrinsic part of the modern history of India as it moves toward its superpower status.

The Vedanta declares, "The Truth and I are One." With that thought and belief, I bow my head in complete surrender to that supreme omnipresent universal energy that is around us, and inside us, whence we came and into which we shall one day certainly merge.

From a scientist and engineer, to business leader, to academician, to philanthropist, and philosopher, and finally to an understanding of self, this has been for me a highly rewarding journey, a journey that merged with the destination until there was no destination left and life became a journey onto itself.

If this book leads you to exploring this new frontier India in all its hues and colors, one part of my duty and Karma will have moved forward.

Vinay Rai

ACKNOWLEDGMENTS

From Vinay Rai

Someone once said that eighty percent of any success is just showing up. The people I am about to acknowledge and thank did much more than just show up.

As a result of this project, I will always consider Bill Simon a very special friend and, in our Indian terminology, Family. He has an extraordinary way of organizing complex material, and an uncanny ability to understand what I wanted to communicate. He wrote under seriously restrictive deadlines, often working late into the night so we could coordinate our conversations. I know he worked especially hard to satisfy my high levels of expectation, and I especially appreciate his calm and fun-loving manner, so in evidence during the time he spent with us in Delhi. In our conversations I realized that, especially with his Jewish background, he absorbed the Hindu philosophy and way of life quite admirably—so much so that he has become half Indian already! I would love to work again with him and perhaps convince him to spend a part of his life in India.

I originally met literary agent Bill Gladstone, the founder and CEO of Waterside Communications, for conversations about setting up a spiritual online university. After these meetings, Bill raised the idea of my writing a book for the American market on India and its global role today. So the inspiration for *Think India* belongs to him.

I started this book with another author, Melissa Rossi, who had to drop out due to time constraints. My thanks to her for her useful inputs and research.

My special thanks to the esteemed Trena Keating, editor in chief of the Dutton imprint at Penguin Group, who not only recognized how valuable this book could be and thus bought it without hesitation but also helped in shaping the work. Her visit to India with her husband, David, added tremendously to the contents, and both Trena and David gave very useful suggestions to the direction of the book and how it could help bring India and its people nearer in understanding to the American audience. Emily Haynes, our editor, went that extra mile to guide the work with her helpful and insightful interventions.

I most sincerely praise and appreciate the work of Paul Joskow, Professor Yasheng Huang, and Abhijit Banerjee, professors at MIT, and Dr. Lant Pritchett, lead socioeconomist of the World Bank, who along with Bill Emmott, formerly of *The Economist,* shared many important insights that inform these pages.

To the overworked officials of the American embassy in India, I extend my appreciation for their valuable input.

My own research team included the painstaking and patient work of Aditi Prasad, Shilpa Sharma, and Ajaita Shah, who, with some friends, chipped in a lot more time and valuable insights.

This is a perfect time to thank my many friends—politicians, academicians, students, businessmen, and professional business executives—for their interviews that gave this book its direction and strength.

From the media, I have nothing but praise for friend Shobhana Bhartia, CEO of the *Hindustan Times,* who generously provided support and photographs used in this book. And the many other media friends who provided useful inputs and background.

My wife and all in my family gave me the moral backing for writing this book, and to them all I extend my deepest expressions of appreciation.

My coauthor's wife is also worthy of my fond appreciation, for Arynne encouraged her husband to travel to India to undertake this book project and has been ever so patient with my midnight and early morning calls.

From William Simon

I saw this book from the start as a challenging but important project. Even more than on any of my previous books, given the schedule, the assistance I received was especially valuable and appreciated.

Vinay ji is surely an ideal coauthor, whose patience I sorely tried. But his strength of conviction and depth of understanding, combined with his articulate ability, made it possible for an outsider like me to understand the beauty of Hinduism and the strengths of India. His generosity during the weeks I spent in the country was of Taj Mahal proportions; our time together added a lifetime of memories to my emotional storehouse. In a truly Indian sense, the generous and hospitable Vinay ji has become a brother.

I also owe a debt of gratitude to Melissa Rossi, whose intensive research contributed immeasurably to this work, and whose apt phrases brighten its pages. Her initial work on this project gave me a platform to work from.

I'm also grateful to the very talented Sheldon Bermont, for his grit, determination, professionalism, and steadfast efforts as he worked behind the scenes; his supportive and insightful wordsmithing have helped make this book what it is.

Aditi Prasad worked diligently and under much pressure to gather the information I needed, supply facts, and write passages. I admire her work and appreciate her efforts. My thanks also to Shilpa Sharma, who was kept so busy attending to my writing needs during my pressure-packed time in India.

Of the many editors I have worked with, the estimable Emily Haynes stands apart as memorable; her guidance and sage advice have helped to shape this book. And my appreciation to Dutton editor in chief Trena Keating, for her belief in this project.

Bill Gladstone, owner of Waterside Communications, my longtime agent and friend, has been thanked by me many times in the past. I continue to be awed by the diverse range of projects he finds for me.

Most of all, I thank my precious wife, who survived my absence without a complaint while Vinay ji and I worked together in Delhi. Arynne's enthusiasm for what she read in my rough drafts was so high that she suggested we consider moving to Delhi from Los Angeles to join the effort of helping this extraordinary nation and its people succeed. Her enthusiastic words helped to keep my encouragement levels high. My prayers now are that she recover speedily from the medical problem that struck her down not long after my return to India. She sits beside me as I write this, a reassurance that she is happily on the mend.

Finally above all, I thank India for the expanded appreciation of life this proud land has given me.

NOTES

Chapter 1

over $23 billion in 2007

11 Poonam Guptal, "Macroeconomic Determinants of Remittances: Evidence from India," International Monetary Fund Working Paper, December 2005.

three percent of the country's GDP

11 Ibid.

Chapter 2

in India rather than China

25 "The McKinsey Global Survey of Business Executives," July 2004.

even faster than the Chinese do

26 *Business Today,* October 8, 2006.

Thirty-two million handsets sold in India

26 Figures from the Telecom Regulator Authority of India (TRAI).

rich and poor continuing to widen
27 *Washington Post*, "India's New Era," Salman Rushdie, May 14, 2004; Page A25 at http://www.washingtonpost.com/wp-dyn/articles/A25770-2004May13.html

ebb and flow of daily life
30 Pavan K. Varma, *Being Indian*. New Delhi: Penguin Books, 2004, p. 73.

quick thinking, cunning, and resolve
30 Ibid., p. 72.

Economist
43 *The Economist*, February 1, 2007.

Chapter 3

Kaun Banega Crorepati
48 Saritha Rai, "In India, a Cable Industry Is Buoyed by a Quiz Show," *New York Times*, August 15, 2005.

India's six million luxury consumers
48 "Consumer Markets in India," (KPMG research with Indian Market Research Bureau) KPMG International, 2005.

$15 billion a year
48 "India Luxury Trends 2006," The Knowledge Company, Technopak Group.

Internet-connecting phones
48 Ibid.

quickly opened nineteen more
48 "Swarovski Plans 19 New Exclusive Stores," *Correspondent*, June 1, 2005.

ten thousand and fifty thousand dollars
52 Marketing Whitebook as quoted in "Consumer Markets in India," KPMG International, 2005.

as high as three hundred million

52 This three hundred million figure, frequently bandied about in the media, is used by the United States of America Department of Commerce, among others; it is often questioned, however.

consumer spending in India

53 NCAER report original.

as they do on food and groceries

54 "India Retail Report 2005," IMAGES-KSA Technopak; figures for 2004.

food and brand-name clothes

54 "A broader audience for song and dance," *The Financial Express*, August 15, 2006.

recently saw revenues triple

54 "A New Face of Youth Consumerism," *Business World*, June 2004.

$375 billion on personal consumption annually

55 "India Retail Report 2005," IMAGES-KSA Technopak.

55 ICICI puts the figure at $292 billion for 2003; Consumer Markets in India, 2005.

14 percent a year

55 Study conducted by Hewitt Associates; Cecily Hall, "Far East— Fashion Forward," *WWW*, June 1, 2006.

fresh basil and thyme

56 Monica Bhide, "As Cash Flows In, Indians Go Out to Eat," *New York Times*, April 20, 2005.

India had a dozen malls

56 "India Retail Report 2005," IMAGES-KSA Technopak.

there were over 150

56 Mall Book 2005—"Retail Real Estate: Malls in India 2005," IMAGES-KSA Technopak.

by the end of 2007

56 Ibid.

via satellite and cable

57   John Sparks, "Why India's Hot. . . . How It's Changing," *Newsweek*, March 6, 2006.

up on the big screen

58   Gabriel Kahn, "India's Bollywood Has a New Focus—Product Placement," *Wall Street Journal*, September 4, 2002.

rose to 1.1 million

61   Society of Indian Automobile manufacturers.

billion phones soon after

62   "India—Fastest-Growing Telecom Market in the World," www.investorideas.com

had not happened before

64   *The Times of India*, February 1, 2007.

target for corn flakes

67   Sala Kannan, "How to Make a Success of Investing in India," *Money Week*, December 19, 2005.

five tons of it by 2001

67   "Crunch Time for Kellogg's," *Business Standard*, November 5, 2001.

yank them the next year

67   Purvita Chatterjee, "Kelloggs says Cheez," *Hindu Business Line*, July 25, 2002.

new factory in Hyderabad

67   Through KSJ India, run in India through Philip Morris India

experiment two years later

68   "Dabur Foods Loses Tang," *The Hindu Business Line*, March 4, 2003.

a hundred more

68   "McDonald's India to Open 100 More Outlets in Next 3 Years," *Hindu Business Line*, July 16, 2006.

protests in Mumbai

68   "Hindu Group Vandalizes McDonald's," AP, April 5, 2001.

50 percent a year

68   Sala Kannan, "How to Make a Success of Investing in India," *Money Week*, December 19, 2005.

$200 billion worth of gold

69   Dianna Farrell and Susan Lund, "Reforming India's Financial System," *McKinsey Quarterly*, 2005 Special Report.

entire country's savings accounts

69   Ibid.

they can make loans

69   Anand Giridharadas, "India Hopes to Wean Citizens from Gold," *International Herald Tribune*, March 16, 2005.

Chapter 4

carefully drilled away

74   Initial findings in 2001 were further supported by excavations in 2006 that found that eleven sets of teeth, believed from 9000 B.C., had been drilled apparently for therapeutic reasons. See Amitabh Avasthi, "9000-Year-Old Drilled Teeth . . . ," *National Geographic News*, April 5, 2006; http://news.nationalgeographic.com/news/2006/04/0405_060405_teeth_drill.html

knowledge and improvement

76   Friedrich Max Müller, "Character of the Hindus," *India: What Can It Teach Us*. New Delhi: Rupa & Co., 2003 (2002), p. 46.

diversity and revering truth

76   Ibid., p. 48.

killed or run out

90   About two million Hindus are in Pakistan today.

which will [then] begin

97   Rabindra Nath Tagore, *Greater India*. New Delhi: Rupa & Co., 2003
      (1909–10) p. 92.

Chapter 5

seventy-five dollars per barrel

101   CNN/USA Today/Gallup poll, conducted February 28–March 1.

Pew Global Attitudes Report

101   "Pew Global Attitudes Report," released in June 2005. According
      to its findings only 23 percent of Pakistanis had a favorable image
      of the United States, while the vast majority (more than 75 per-
      cent) viewed America and its foreign policies unfavorably. In
      sharp contrast, 71 percent of the Indian populace had a favorable
      image of the United States and its policies in 2005. http://pewglobal
      .org/reports/display.php?PageID=824

civilian nukes

102   Alex Perry, "Let's Be Friends," *Time Magazine*, February 26, 2006.

naval vessels

103   CNN.com, "U.S. to Boost Arms Sales to India," March 2, 2006,
      http://www.cnn.com/2006/WORLD/asiapcf/03/02/bush.india.fri/
      index.html

against a third country

104   Sun Yuxi in an interview with *Calcutta Telegraph*. http://www
      .csmonitor.com/2005/0408/p05s01-woap.html

wrung from the British

107   The then U.S. Ambassador to India, William Phillips, so forcefully
      backed the nationalist cause and so movingly conveyed to President
      Roosevelt India's feeling of powerlessness under the Raj that the
      British government immediately blacklisted him, publicly and offi-
      cially labeling him persona non grata and forcing him out of the
      post. Even the U.S. Congress jumped in, lambasting British Prime

Minister Churchill for trying to suppress the movement and imprisoning freedom fighters Gandhi and Nehru. The topic created such a furor that numerous op-ed pieces and letters to the editors filled the pages of the most prestigious American newspapers as the British tried to defend their actions in India, although soon enough they too had to admit it was time to cut the cords.

looks like a Communist to me
108 See "Transcriptions of Conversations Between Justice William O. Douglas and Professor Walter F. Murphy," June 5, 1963. http://info share1.princeton.edu/libraries/firestone/rbsc/finding_aids/douglas/douglas16.html

self-sufficient in food production
109 Noah Zerbe, "Feeding the Famine: American Food Aid and the GMO Debate in South Africa," Center for Philosophy of Law, Catholic University of Louvain. http://www.geocities.com/nzerbe/pubs/famine.pdf

secret negotiations with China
110 Foreign Relations, 1969–1976, Volume XI, South Asia Crisis, 1971, at http://www.state.gov/r/pa/ho/frus/nixon/xi/45650.htm

Soviet pressure
110 See "India and America, Improving an Uneasy Relationship," Ajay Kamalakaran. June 22, 2004. Media Monitors Network, http://usa.mediamonitors.net/headlines/india_and_america_improving_an_uneasy_relationship

high-technology sales to India
111 Kennith J. Conboy, "A Guide to U.S.–South Asian Relations," the Heritage Foundation, October 14, 1988.

France, Germany, and Russia
113 "New Priorities in South Asia: U.S. Policy Toward India, Pakistan, and Afghanistan," Chairman's Report of an independent task force, cosponsored by the Council on Foreign Relations and the Asia Society, October 2003. http://www.asiasociety.org/policy_business/india-southasia10-30-03.pdf

a partner of great value

114 "New Priorities in South Asia: U.S. Policy Toward India, Pakistan and Afghanistan," op. cit.

every reason to welcome

116 Baker Spring, "Nuclear Energy Cooperation with India Will Strengthen US-India Ties," Heritage Research, the Heritage Foundation, June 20, 2006. http://www.heritage.org/Research/Asia andthePacific/upload/em_1007.pdf

Geoffrey Pyatt

116 Geoffrey Pyatt, deputy chief of mission, U.S. Embassy in India, in an interview with the author, September 27, 2006.

strategically stable Asia

117 "National Security Strategy of the USA," September 2002. http://www.globalsecurity.org/military/library/policy/national/nss-020920.pdf

third in defense spending

118 Richard P. Lawless, deputy undersecretary of defense, testimony before the Subcommittee on East Asian and Pacific Affairs, Committee on Foreign Relations, U.S. Senate, April 26, 2004. http://foreign.senate.gov/testimony/2004/LawlessTestimony040422.pdf

Sri Lanka into its orbit

118 Paramjit Sinha, "US-India Defense Ties," *Asian Affairs*, June 2006. http://www.asianaffairs.com/june2006/us_india.htm

Global 2020 Report

119 "Mapping the Global Future" is the third unclassified report prepared by the National Intelligence Council (NIC) in the past seven years that takes a long-term view of the future. The NIC, as a center of strategic thinking and over-the-horizon analysis for the U.S. government, aims to provide U.S. policy makers with a view of how world developments could evolve, identifying opportunities and potentially negative outcomes that might warrant policy action. http://www.dni.gov/nic/NIC_globaltrend2020.html

taking over again from government

119 "Mapping the Global Future," report of the National Intelligence Council's 2020 Project. http://www.dni.gov/nic/NIC_globaltrend 2020.html

threatening U.S. interests

120 "The Rising Economic Clout of China," *The Christian Science Monitor*, June 30, 2005. http://www.csmonitor.com/2005/0630/p01s01-usec.html

Mussolini or Francisco Franco

120 Richard Bernstein and Ross H. Munro, "China: The Coming Conflict with America," *Foreign Affairs*, Vol. 76, No. 2, March/April 1997, p. 27.

same bed, different dreams

120 David M. Lampton, *Same Bed, Different Dreams: Managing US-China Relations 1989–2000*. California: University of California Press, 2001, p. ix.

low-impact nation

121 Jasjit Singh in an interview for this author's previous book *Rethinking India*.

Sino-India relations

122 M. V. Rappai, "India-China Relations and the Nuclear Realpolitik," *Strategic Analysis*, Volume 23, No. 1, April 1999.

K. Santhanam

124 Interview with Rahul Pandita for *Rethinking India*.

discuss this publicly

124 Sultan Shahin, "India: The Game the Pentagon Plays," http://www.atimes.com/atimes/South_Asia/EG12Df05.html

low-end operations

124 See "America-India and the Outsourcing of Imperial Overreach," Siddhartha Vardarajan, Global Research, July 2005. http://www.globalresearch.ca/index.php?context=viewArticle&code=VAR2005 0719&articleId=711

$64 million in 2005

125   Christopher Griffin, "What India Wants," *Armed Forces Journal*.
      http://www.afji.com/2006/05/1667683/

2003 Knowledge@Wharton report

126   "Does China Pose an Economic Threat to the United States?"
      December 13, 2003.

Chapter 6

exports and imports

136   "Israel Favours India in Expanded UNSC," *The Hindustan Times*,
      November 4, 2006, quoting Israeli Ambassador to India David
      Daniele.

Palestinian cause

135   See "India and Israel United in Defense," Sudha Ramachandran,
      Asia Times Online, June 26, 2002. http://www.atimes.com/ind-pak/
      DF26Df02.html

the Financial Times

136   A 2003 *Financial Times* report appearing on Yale Global Online,
      http://yaleglobal.yale.edu/display.article?id=2411

much-hyped visit

136   Ariel Sharon in September 2003, became the first Israeli prime min-
      ister to visit India since the two nations established full diplomatic
      relations in 1992.

expanding naval power

137   "Global Trends 2020 Report," prepared by the National Intelligence
      Council. http://www.odni.gov/nic/NIC_globaltrend2020_s2.html

the country's own resources

137   J. Nandakumar, "India, China and Energy Security," EnergyPulse,
      June 2004. http://www.energypulse.net/centers/article/article_print
      .cfm?a_id=761; see also "Energy Consumption by End-User Sec-

tor," the IEO2006 projections http://www.eia.doe.gov/oiaf/ieo/pdf/
enduse.pdf.

10 percent by 2020

137   "India's Energy Security Challenge," Institute for Analysis of Global
Security.

close and friendly relations

139   Indian Prime Minister's statement on Iran, Indian Parliament, February 17, 2006. http://pmindia.nic.in/lspeech.asp?id=279

balance to China's heft

140   "Lee Kuan Yew Reflects," *Time* magazine online, http://www.time
.com/time/asia/covers/501051212/lky_intvu.html

hosted a seminar in 2003

143   "Prospects of India-Russia Security Relations," seminar hosted
by the Carnegie Endowment for International Peace. http://www
.carnegieendowment.org/events/index.cfm?fa=eventDetail&id=591

renewing once tight ties

144   "Putin Calls on Old Friend India," *Forbes.* http://www.forbes.com/
facesinthenews/2007/01/29/putin-india-singh-face-lead-cx_rd_0128
autofacescan02.html

voyage of discovery

146   "India Prime Minister Dr. Manmohan Singh's Statement at the Joint
Conference with President Luiz Inacio of Brazil," September 13,
2006. http://pib.nic.in/release/release.asp?relid=20653&kwd=

anything they want

151   Tenzin Tsundue, "Between the Dragon and the Elephant," *The Economic Times,* January 2, 2005.

Chapter 7

all the time

160   "Excerpts from a Conversation with Carrière," July 2006. http://
       www.lifepositive.com/Mind/culture/indology/mahabharata.asp

Dominique Lapierre

166   Author of many a bestseller including *Freedom at Midnight* (on In-
       dia's history) and *City of Joy* (on Calcutta's slum dwellers).

driving its society forward

166   Dominique Lapierre, "OK Tata Truckland," *Outlook*, Independence
       Day Special, August 21, 2006, p. 50.

remote rural villages

167   "Small Towns, Huge Donations," *The Times of India*, May 21, 2006.

different social realities

167   Amartya Sen, *The Argumentative Indian: Writings on Indian History,
       Culture and Identity*. London: Penguin Books, 2005, p. 35.

high spiritual truths

170   http://www.hinduwisdom.info/thoughts.htm

Mahabharata and refer to it

171   "Excerpts From a Conversation With Carrière." http://www.life
       positive.com/Mind/culture/indology/mahabharata.asp

Oriental-travel memoirs

173   Henri Michaux, *Un Barbare en Asie*. Paris: Gallimard, 1967 (1933),
       p. 83. Translated by resident French professor at the School of Lan-
       guages, Rai Foundation, New Delhi.

bustling human contact

175   Stanley Wolpert, *An Introduction to India*. New Delhi: Penguin
       Books, 1994, p. 134.

St. Stephen's

178   *The Times of India*, August 30, 2006. p. 7.

lack of knowledge

178   Friedrich Max Müller, "Character of the Hindus," *India: What Can It Teach Us*, New Delhi: Rupa & Co., 2003 (2002), pp. 47–48.

big or small—was made

178   "Mumbai Disputes Rudest City Tag," BBC News, Mumbai. http://news.bbc.co.uk/2/hi/south_asia/5103914.stm

clear to any Indian

179   Gitanjali Kolanad, *Cultureshock! India,* Singapore: Marshall Cavendish editions, 2005, p. 237.

Chapter 9

35 percent in 2007

214   Jeffrey Sachs, *End of Poverty*. p. 182.

as early as 1952

215   Population Reference Bureau article, Carl Haub, March 2002.

from six children per woman to three

215   "United Nations World Population Prospects," 2006.

by the age of eighteen

216   2006 World Population Data Sheets, Population Reference Bureau.

the rate is still 3.4

216   Ibid.

from rural to urban settings

216   Jeffrey Sachs, *End of Poverty*. pp. 36-37.

former health ministers

217   http://www.overpopulation.com/articles/2001/000085.html

17 percent

217   Jeffrey Sachs, *End of Poverty*. p. 174.

formal education at all
218   The National Family Health Survey-3, conducted in 29 states be-
       tween December 2005 and August 2006.

more than $4 billion
223   http://www.expressindia.com/fullstory.php?newsid=67159

connection to the power grid
226   www.tve.org/ho/doc.cfm?aid=1676&lang=English

Spain, the United States, and Denmark
226   www.rediff.com/money/2005/mar/29wind.htm

prescribed for their crimes
228   Bibek Debroy, "ICT and Poverty", in *Integrating the Rural Poor into
       Markets*, ed. Bibek Debroy and Amir Ullah Khan, p. 255

back to the books
234   http://www.ashanet.org/nycnj/events/2002/20020129-indiventure/
       projects/train.htm

experience of the IT sector
235   http://www.mindtree.com/kc/wpa.php#

one half of our nation shining
236   http://hindustantimes.com/news/specials/leadership2006/coverage_
       17110609.shtml

Chapter 10

boost growth as well
242   Diana Farrell, "Who Wins in Offshoring?" *International Herald Tri-
       bune*, February 7, 2004.

INDEX

Note: Page numbers in *italics* refer to illustrations.